Terry Tan

Cooking with Chinese Herbs

TIMES EDITIONS

Managing Editor: Jamilah Mohd Hassan
Editor: Selina Kuo
Designer: Tan Shiang Chin
Photographer: Edmond Ho
Food Stylist: Christopher Tan
Production Co-ordinator: Nor Sidah Haron

© 1983 Times Editions Private Limited
© 2003 Times Media Private Limited
© 2004 Marshall Cavendish International (Asia) Private Limited

First published 1983
Reprinted 1983, 1988, 1990, 1993, 1996, 2003
Limp edition 2003
This new edition 2004

Published by Times Editions – Marshall Cavendish
An imprint of Marshall Cavendish International (Asia) Private Limited
A member of the Times Publishing Limited
Times Centre, 1 New Industrial Road, Singapore 536196
Tel: (65) 6213 9288   Fax: (65) 6285 4871
E-mail: te@sg.marshallcavendish.com
Online Bookstore: http://www.timesone.com.sg/te

Malaysian Office:
Federal Publications Sdn Bhd (General & Reference Publishing) (3024-D)
Times Subang
Lot 46, Subang Hi-Tech Industrial Park
Batu Tiga, 40000 Shah Alam
Selangor Darul Ehsan, Malaysia
Tel: (603) 5635 2191   Fax: (603) 5635 2706
E-mail: cchong@tpg.com.my

National Library Board (Singapore) Cataloguing in Publication Data

Tan, Terry
Cooking with Chinese herbs / Terry Tan. – New ed. – Singapore: Times Editions, 2004.
p. cm.
ISBN 981-232-960-9

1. Cookery, Chinese. 2. Cookery (Herbs) I. Title.

TX724.5.C5
641.5951 — dc21   SLS2004028082

Printed in Singapore by Times Printers Pte Ltd

Acknowledgements

The author wishes to thank Christopher Tan
for his cooking and styling efforts and
Dr. Geng Yu Ling for her recipes and professional input
as a Traditional Chinese Medicine (TCM) practitioner.

contents

foreword

For thousands of years, within the pantheon of revered Chinese culinary practices, the school of herbal cooking has always been cherished for its restorative elements and hearty prescription for every human ill. Soups, stews and teas that have curative promise are legion and deemed to effectively restore *Qi* and to correct any bodily imbalance. The founding tenet of Traditional Chinese Medicine (TCM), under which herbal brews are a respected and revered school, points to this very imbalance that causes many human ills. Herbal foods may be regarded as being primarily preventative, underscoring the adage "prevention is better then cure". It is by this dictum that we should regard herbal cooking — as an ancient and time-honoured branch of Chinese cuisine that fathoms the efficacy of a multitude of herbs, barks, roots, nuts and seeds when paired with meat, poultry, vegetables or seafood. Even for skeptics chary of this claim, there is the undeniable fact of sheer tastiness.

A distinction is to be made between specific medicinal preparations in TCM and herbal ones that transform everyday dishes into powerhouses of sustenance. While the former can be distasteful to those unused to strong and even foul flavours, the range of herbs used in this book are generally milder and used in judicious tandem with familiar meats and vegetables.

In this school of cooking, little is added by way of artificial flavourings as the intention is to let the herbs do the work. Those unaccustomed to such dishes may initially find them strange, but when the healthy promise behind each blend has been felt, a willing acceptance will follow. Rest assured that there are no dire consequences to be feared in enjoying duck with bitter apricot kernels; chicken with Chinese wolfberries; or pork with Chinese angelica, or *dang gui* as it is better known in Mandarin. With this book, it will be possible for even the most diffident of cooks to produce a wide spectrum of delicious and wholesome dishes, not to mention there is much room for adaptation and innovation even within the fairly rigid framework that governs herbal mixes. Regard this book as a vital entry to your library of good eating tomes, adding to the richness that is Chinese cuisine. It will certainly enrich your table, whatever the efficacious promise.

introduction

Setting out to write this book proved a formidable challenge. Up until that point, the little I knew about herbal mixes was mostly limited to what my parents once coaxed me to drink or eat in a bid to restore my balance of Yin and Yang (see *Yin-Yang Philosophy and Food*). The prospect of rooting out recipes from old aunts, herbalists, friends and seasoned practitioners of herbal cooking was excitingly delicious, if uphill some of the way. Some herbalists to whom I spoke were not exactly forthcoming, although many others were. Over many months, I learnt to appreciate the profound and tasty promise of such dishes as chicken with ginseng soup; braised duck with lotus seeds; and mutton with the somewhat mystical cordyceps (*dong zhong xia chao*). That said, there is really no deep mystery about Chinese herbal cooking. One need only have faith in an ancient discipline that millions of Chinese already subscribe to with fervour.

In revamping my original publication, I have had the distinct advantage of receiving advice from Dr. Geng Yu Ling (M.Sc.), a TCM practitioner and herbalist registered with the TCM Association (UK) and based in London for the past eight years. Dr. Geng is also a medical doctor and specialist in internal medicine. She sought TCM training in Beijing University after completing her clinical studies in her hometown of Hubei. I had first seen Dr. Geng for a pesky bladder problem. Despite several specialists in London, I was still like a leaky bucket and had been for more than two decades. She diagnosed my problem as "dysfunctional kidneys" and prescribed a course of treatment involving cordyceps. Within two months, my problem vanished. I have always had faith in TCM and this served only to reinforce it. Dr. Geng has also been instrumental in providing much background information on every dish in this book. From her, I have learnt so much more about herbalism.

the semantics of herbal cooking

The Chinese herbal ingredients used in this book are without overpowering odours that characterise many blends and poultices often slapped on festering sores. Neither are they evil-smelling brews from a fumy cauldron frothing with medicinal mixes. The world and a half today have come to realise that many of the thousands of dried barks, seeds, nuts and herbs traditionally used in TCM treatment also lend themselves to a range of everyday dishes that are the better for their inclusion.

It is not easy for those uninitiated to fully learn all the health implications in each blend of herbs, complex or simple, as most of such knowledge has been handed down by word of mouth over centuries. What is of paramount importance, then, is that herbal brews are concocted according to individual body constitutions, as well as physical and emotional states. The TCM practitioner seeks to get at the root of the problem rather than the symptom and believes that there can be no panacea for all ills.

TCM dictates that illnesses can be caused by one factor or a combination of several; externally, these are heat, dampness and dryness, and internally, they encompass more than just physical dysfunction to include the effects of happiness, anger, anxiety, grief, fear and trauma, as well as injuries, minor wounds, and over-indulgence. It is, therefore, wise to avoid foods that are extreme in taste, be they spicy, salty, sweet and etc.

In TCM, individual foods are also believed to have characteristics that affect the human constitution. The list here is long and has been broken down into notes preceding the relevant recipes. Suffice to say, for now, that herbal cooking is classically categorised according to poultry, meat, seafood and vegetable dishes, as well as soups and teas.

Poultry such as duck and goose provide meat that is protein-rich but also overly fatty, and so should be eaten sparingly by people who suffer from obesity, hypertension, and heart or cholesterol problems. Chicken is regarded as neutral in energy and when combined with either 'hot' or 'cold' herbs take on the characteristics of the accompanying herbal blend. Of all the meats used in herbal cooking, mutton or lamb is oft used for its stimulating and strengthening properties. For seafood, fish is rich in protein but many types of shellfish have the added nuisance of being cholesterol-rich and, hence, should be avoided or used judiciously.

The study of herbs goes back some 3,000 years to the second dawn of Chinese civilization, when history was beginning to be chronicled and ancient analects recorded. In those early writings, references were made to cooked herbs, and hundreds believed to have curative and restorative powers were named. It was not until 1518, during the Ming Dynasty, however, that medicinal knowledge accrued from research and experimentation performed in centuries past were compiled into one book, and by one man. Li Shi Zhen spent most of his adult life endeavouring the onerous task of recording the preventative, diagnostic and curative principles of natural medication. His efforts resulted in the first ever encyclopaedia of Chinese herbs — *Ben Cao Gang Mu* or the *Compendium of Materia Medica*. Li's admirable work detailed the use of some 1,800 herbs, roots, barks, seeds, plants and nuts, and remains to this day the guiding light for all Chinese physicians. By the seventeenth century, the learned tome had found its way to Japan via traders and seafarers, and some years later, it was translated into Japanese. To date, it has been translated into languages including German, French, Korean and Russian.

In as early as the Tang Dynasty, a medical training institute known as the Imperial Medical College, the first of its kind, was set up in the Middle Kingdom. Since then, a legion of men and women have been schooled in diagnosis based on the principles of universal balance and the application of herbal medicine for a wide spectrum of human ills.

in history

the roots of sustenance

In primitive times, much of rural China lived on the brink of hunger and the populace sought sustenance in any and every way they could. Farming was, at that time, still a millennium away and hunting was a discouraging struggle in Nature's patch. Traditional sources of food were, in their order of importance, plants, animals and what lay beneath the soil.

Through the ensuing centuries, the people learnt to differentiate between edible and poisonous varieties of roots, barks and seeds, but not before Nature's toxic produce claimed many lives. The deaths, while unfortunate, were not in vain as they became invaluable lessons in identifying poisons and, later, antidotes. Thus was born today's daunting legacy of medicinal blends and practice of incorporating herbs into daily meals.

Perhaps to say the protracted documentation of Chinese herbs and, in particular, their treatment of maladies grew from knowledge gained in those uncertain and unrecorded times.

In any case, the line between medicinal efficacy and culinary delicacy grew only thinner with time, as the purposes of food, nourishment and curative effect meshed and merged. As Chinese cuisine evolved, herbs became more and more inextricably linked with everyday foods. There is certainly more to the adage "medicine and food come from the same source" than we realise.

Herbal dishes are customarily double-boiled, braised or steamed and rarely, if ever, fried. Fat, in fact, is reduced to a minimum in herbal cooking. There is also a certain clarity of flavours, which is the result of allowing the natural tastes and smells of the chosen ingredients to come through unadulterated and unmasked by a barrage of seasonings. It remains the cornerstone of Chinese herbalism that while a headache can be relieved with an analgesic, it is best remedied by attaining overall, physical well-being through the frequent consumption of this herbal soup or that herbal stew. Herbal cooking is a classic cuisine in its own right, and with increased creativity in the field, the experience of herbal foods will, no doubt, be taken far beyond the sometimes stodgy medicinal realm. In the very least, it will make for tasty, wholesome nutrition and, with help from this book, even fine dining at times.

yin-yang philosophy and food

When interest in Feng Shui swept over parts of the world in recent years, in its shadow resided, more basically, principles of Yin and Yang. Yin-Yang theory has long since informed Chinese thought and beliefs, although some strict modernists will continue to regard it as mystical nonsense. In traditional Chinese culture, everything boils down to the opposing forces of Yin and Yang. The former, in broad strokes, represents the Moon, Earth, female gender and darkness, as well as the negative properties of coldness, passivity and softness. The latter, at the other end of the spectrum, represents the Sun, Heaven, male gender and light, as well as such properties as heat, activity and hardness. The ultimate and deceptively simple objective is to strike a perfect balance between the opposing forces by aiding their mutual interaction. In a crass generalisation, then, a person harbouring elements or a state of 'coldness' can counter the condition by eating 'hot' foods and, likewise, elements of 'heat' can be countered by drinking 'cooling' brews, or brews made from 'cold' herbs.

Creating a blend of herbs that complements everyday ingredients to achieve balanced Yin and Yang is an art a lot more complex than many realise. Good herbalists know not only how to make blends that have all the right herbs in the right proportions, but also how much of meat, poultry, seafood or vegetables to use in relation to each blend. Bearing in mind that the counteracting properties of the herbs have to mesh perfectly not only with one another, but also with those of the common ingredients, and altogether with the body that consumes them to produce the internal, Yin-Yang equilibrium that is so craved.

So pervaded is Chinese food and nutrition by concepts of Yin and Yang, however, that regard for the opposing forces is not limited to the relationship between one's body and the ingestion of categorically 'hot', 'cold' and 'neutral' foods. In fact, the influence of Yin-Yang extends to cooking and the creation of tastes. By the laws of Yin and Yang, the flavour of a dish should be the balanced sum of opposites and no one flavour should be unabashedly forward. It would be nearly impossible now to not mention the universally loved sweet-and-sour formula, arguably the Big Mac of Chinese food in the world. In it, vinegar, which is considered a negative element for its sourness, is countered and harmonised with some sugar. It is this insistence on balance that makes Chinese cuisine what it is — a totally logical

weights and measures

Most dried herbs are extremely light and traditional herbalists would use the old-fashioned *daching* or Chinese balance to determine quantities that are too slight for the common scales. Although digital scales are increasingly assuming the role of the *daching* into the twenty-first century, many herbalists continue to rely on a combination of skill and instinct in determining how much of each herb is needed for a given blend. Despite the seeming imprecision, few are known to have rejected the expertise of a herbalist in favour of doing their own measuring and blending of ingredients. As for the volume of liquid that accompanies a herbal blend, the age-old practice of measuring by the number of Chinese soup bowls often still applies. In the pursuit of clarity, however, all liquid measures in this book have been metricised.

storing herbs

All dried herbs, barks, seeds and nuts should be stored in jars with tight-fitting lids. It is not a good idea to use opaque containers as any deterioration would not be immediately noticed. Use clear glass jars instead, but keep them away from strong sunlight. Remember, also, that cooking fumes are easily absorbed by dried herbs, so keep them away from where they are susceptible.

the a-y of chinese herbs

The glossary here lists the herbs in their English names, which are accompanied by their Mandarin names in *han yu pin yin and phonetically spelt Cantonese names. Refer to the chart at the end of this glossary for the corresponding botanical names, as well as Mandarin names in Chinese characters.*

Sweet apricot kernels

Herbal shops stock two types of apricot kernels: *bei xing*, the bitter, northern variety, and *nan xing*, the sweet, southern variety. The former are smaller and rounder than the latter and most Chinese herbalists are likely to identify them as bitter and sweet almonds respectively. Both are usually used at the same time, and in equal proportions.

Apricot kernels
(xing ren/hung ngan)
Also known as "Chinese almonds", kernels of the Mongolian apricot, are also found in the former Manchuria and the northern Chinese provinces of Hebei, Beijing and Shandong. In Korea, it is used as an expectorant and a remedy for dry throats, lung diseases and laryngitis. In China and Japan, it is regarded as a sedative for respiratory problems, a tonic and remedy for severe colds, asthma, rheumatism, swollen feet and constipation. In Indochina, a special preparation of the smashed fruit is chewed but not swallowed, to protect the bronchial tubes from cold during winter.

Astralagus root
(huang qi/puk kei)
Found in Korea and the northern Chinese provinces of Shanxi and Gansu, the pale yellow roots are believed to be good for the treatment of poor blood circulation and fatigue.

Bitter apricot kernels

More than any other, the chrysanthemum rose from relative obscurity to become known as a universal balm believed to be efficacious for a whole host of ailments. These range from a weak liver to poor eyesight, bad circulation, infections, digestive upsets, nervous disorders, menstrual irregularity, greying hair and unhealthy blood.

The plants are in full flower in November; this explains their profusion during the Chinese New Year season in January. The flowering branches are picked, tied into neat bundles, hung upside down and dried in the shade. The dried heads are then cut off, bleached with sulphur gas, put at once into the sunshine and air and shaken in a large sieve so that the heads become rounded.

The two most used species are the *chrysanthemum indicum*, which grows wild in most parts of China except the cold north, and the *chrysanthemum morifolium*, commonly cultivated in pots in Singapore and other parts of Southeast Asia, as well as in the Chinese provinces of Anhui and Zhejiang.

Codonopsis root

Codonopsis root (*dang shen/dong sam*)

Two species of the root exist — one is a native of the region consisting of the former Manchuria and the northern China, namely the provinces of Inner Mongolia and Qinghai; while the other originated from Qinghai but has come to be cultivated in the central Chinese provinces of Sichuan and Hubei. The root is generally used as a tonic and stimulant reputedly good for the treatment of gonorrhea, blood circulation and gynaecological diseases. In some parts of Asia, it is widely adopted as a respectable substitute for the more expensive ginseng. Herbal medicine researchers have recorded that the extract of the codonopsis root can increase the number of red corpuscles and reduce the number of leucocytes in the blood. The codonopsis root is sometimes mistakenly identified and believed to be the mid-section of ginseng.

Cordyceps (*dong chong xia cao/tung chung cho*)

The cordycep's Mandarin name, *dong zhong xia cao*, literally translates into "worms in winter, grass in summer". Indeed, the cordycep begins life as a lowly worm that creeps about in winter, undergoes metamorphosis through spring to become a plant in summer, and dries up to fall like a shrivelled twig in autumn. It is the shrivelled twigs that are collected as cordyceps. They are found mainly in China, specifically in the provinces of Sichuan, Qinghai, Guizhou and Yunnan, and only experts with the well-honed powers of truffle hunters can pinpoint the exact underground lair of hibernation.

The cordycep certainly looks like a mummified creepy-crawly with tiny, black, beady eyes that apparently fill with life when the cordycep is put to the boil. As an ingredient reputedly vital to the well-being of one's physical make-up, the cordycep is believed to rejuvenate and reinstate life's vigour by virtue of its incredible resilience, as well as improve lumbago and general debility.

Eucommia bark (*du zhong/dou chong*)

A bark found in the Chinese provinces of Sichuan, Shanxi, Hubei and Henan, it is believed to have a tonic effect on the liver, kidneys, bones and ligaments. It is widely used to treat backache, hypertension and cases of threatened miscarriage.

The bark is peeled in spring and early summer but the tree is never girdled because that would kill it. The pieces of bark are then folded with the inner surfaces together, tied with rice straw and left to 'sweat' for a week. When the inner surfaces are brownish-black, the bark is untied, flattened and dried in the sun. Silver-white threads are revealed when the coarse outer part is scraped off or when the bark is cracked. The extract obtained from pounding the bark, when consumed with wine or pork, is believed to be good for the liver, kidneys and spleen. It is also believed to be something of an aphrodisiac. Eucommia bark is always used in a mixture, and never by itself.

Euryale seeds (*qian shi/see sat*)
These come from a plant that is cultivated in India, China and Japan. Although literature indicates that all parts of the plant are considered to be tonic and astringent, only the seeds are used. Hard, brown, and looking rather like barley grains, euryale seeds take on a flower-like shape when boiled. Believed to be good for diseases of the spleen and the treatment of gonorrhea, the seeds are generally served in the form of a sweet that also features longans.

Foxglove root (treated)

Foxglove root (treated) (*shou di huang/sok dei*)
Foxglove root comes in two varieties: treated and untreated. The Mandarin and Cantonese names of the treated variety literally translates into "cooked earth", and pieces of the root are rather nondescript in appearance: black and hardened clumps. The plant is grown in northern and northwestern China, and it is the tuberous root or rhizome that is used. In its fresh and untreated form, the root is called *sheng di huang* in Mandarin or *sang dei* in Cantonese, both of which translate into "raw earth". To 'cook' the earth, as it were, pieces of the root are dried in a kiln. Foxglove root is believed to be good for the treatment of cough, headache, vertigo, low blood pressure, backache, threatened miscarriage, inflamed eyes and anaemia, as well as disorders of the kidneys and lungs.

Gingko nuts (*bai guo/bak gor*)
Smooth ivory shells enclosing nuggets of buttery and bitter-sweet flavour, gingko nuts are veritable culinary chameleons. They have an elusive quality about them, a taste that is at once mysterious and yet familiar, rather like perfumed almonds with a slightly bitter aftertaste. They are native to Japan and in the Chinese provinces of Guangxi, Sichuan and Henan.

Gingko nuts are good for asthma, coughs, gynaecological problems, bladder ailments and urinary disorders. An extract of the fruit is supposed to have a strongly deterrent effect on the growth of bacteria causing tuberculosis. Young fruits with their fleshy green outer portion are soaked in rapeseed oil and then consumed as a remedy for tuberculosis.

The nuts are sold shelled and unshelled. Unshelled nuts keep well for up to a few months before they become susceptible to a weevil that reduces each nut to pale dust. Shelled nuts can be refrigerated and kept up to a few weeks. To prepare unshelled nuts, give each a sharp tap on the tapered edge with a small hammer or similarly heavy object. Be careful not to use too much force as the soft nut inside can end up bruised or, worse, broken.

Once cracked, soak or boil for a few minutes until the brown skin, which is slightly caustic, can be rubbed off easily.

Preparation does not end with cleaned, shelled nuts, even if you have been lucky enough to find them in the supermarket, there is still the fiddly chore of removing the bitter cores that are as fine as needles. To remove cores, push a fine toothpick or skewer through each nut, from the base right through to the other, tapered end. Thus prepared, cook as you would any vegetable.

Korean ginseng

Chinese ginseng

American ginseng

Ginseng

This strange-looking root has been held in the highest regard by the Chinese and other Asians for hundreds of years. In the world of medicinal herbs, no other product quite matches its formidable reputation for restorative powers, a point that seems to draw more believers than skeptics. In the very least, it is something of an enigma for sheer price alone. You can buy ginseng for a few dollars a root or you could fork out $60,000 for another not much different looking. Such is the mystique of ginseng and its alleged curative powers. How ginseng came to earn and keep its reputation (and price tag) has more versions than the root has secondary roots. The most interesting account, by far, tells of an old Chinese farmer who was at death's door one cold winter night, drank a brew of ginseng and recovered almost instantly to till for a good many more years. The farmer is believed to have drunk the most powerful ginseng of all, reputedly found only in northern China.

Into the twenty-first century, ginseng is widely accepted as belonging to one of three main types — Chinese ginseng (*ren shen/yan sam*); American ginseng (*yang shen/ yong sam*); and Korean ginseng (*gao li shen/go lai sam*). American ginseng is sometimes also known as the 'flower-flag' ginseng (*hua qi shen/fa kei sam*) because Chinese of the past likened the numerous stars on the American flag to flowers. Despite what the traditionalists seek to uphold, it is safe to say today that no one type of ginseng is necessarily better than the other. Within each type of ginseng, however, are many grades, and it is the grade of the ginseng that matters more. Also, the name of the root no longer indicates the geographical origins of the root, but only its species. The lucrative promise of the revered root has spurred growers around the world to try their hand at cultivating any faintly profitable

species of ginseng. China, to that end, is the world's largest exporter of American ginseng. Far less important than where the root comes from is how it came to be; wild ginseng is always infinitely more valuable than its farmed counterpart.

Much research has been done on the most famous of Chinese herbs in an effort to discover the secrets that reside within. Since the mid-twentieth century, the root has been thoroughly examined and several physiologically active substances have been isolated — in particular *panaxin* which increases muscular tone; *panax acid* which improves metabolism and the vascular system; *panaquilon* which influences the endocrine system; *panacen* which stimulates the nerve centres; and *ginsenin* which is supposed to be beneficial for diabetes sufferers — thereby lending some strength to the once disputed beliefs that ginseng invigorates and also encourages healing processes in the body after illness, but perhaps not to the degree of reviving a near dying man, as it reputedly did the farmer.

Hasma (*xue ge/shuet kup*)

Hasma refers to the glands of northern snow frogs that are dried and then sold in the form of brown, crumb-like bits. The crumbs must be soaked in water to soften before use and turn into white, cotton-like clumps with soaking.

Hyacinth beans
(*bian dou/been dau*)

Also known as the Egyptian kidney bean, the hyacinth bean has a far less exotic name in Mandarin — *bian dou*, which literally means "flat bean". Widely cultivated in the tropics and sub-tropics, the hyacinth flower is picked just as it is opening, usually in August or September, and then dried in the shade. The bean is sweet and slightly warming, and is prescribed for such discomforts as summer heat disorders, dysentery and bloody stools. On the Malay Peninsula, the Malays sometimes use the leaves to make a poultice for eczema and to treat earache. In Indonesia, water added to the juice from crushed leaves, with a little fennel, is strained and drunk as a 'coolant'.

Lily bulb petals
(*bai he/bak hup*)

The bulbs are harvested from July to September, then separated, blanched, dried and bleached in sulphur fumes. Lily bulb petals are believed to be beneficial for an extraordinary range of illnesses, from pulmonary diseases and ulcers to coughs and dry throats.

Longan flesh
(*long yan rou/long ngan yok*)

Longan, a name derived from its Mandarin and Cantonese counterparts, which literally mean "dragon's eye", is a small, seasonal fruit that comes in bunches. In its fresh form, each longan fruit is about the size of a grape and has a semi-hard, greenish-brown shell. The flesh beneath is sweet, succulent and translucent and holds at its centre a round, dark brown seed; which is how a shelled longan could resemble an eye. A native of East Asia, longan is cultivated in China and parts of Indochina. Herbalists, however, only ever stock dried longans, which come in two forms — in their shells, with stones intact, or ready-shelled as lumps of tightly packed longan flesh. Most herbal shops sell longan flesh that is dark brown in colour. Of late, small, orange-brown Taiwanese dried longans are also being sold. These yield lighter-coloured, more delicately flavoured brews. Much prized in China for its warming and tonic properties, longan flesh is considered to be good for the spleen, heart, kidneys, lungs and mental faculties. It is also prescribed to treat nervous disorders with the powdered kernel used as a styptic.

Lotus root (*lian ou jie/leen ngau*)

This rhizome is from the same plant that gives us lotus seeds and is eaten widely by Asians either fresh or dried. Not strictly a herb, it is nonetheless regarded with a degree of respect within Chinese herbal cooking. The fresh form can be bought covered with mud in wet markets or scrubbed cleaned from supermarkets. Lotus roots look like large tubers, each with numerous holes running down their length and look like perforated pieces of marrow when sliced. Cooked with meat in soups and stews, it is believed to be good for the treatment of diabetes, irregular menstrual flow, constipation and stress. Younger rhizomes contain a starch that is similar to arrowroot and is boiled to a thin porridge to relieve diarrhoea and dysentery.

Lotus seeds (*lian zi/leen chi*)

Lotus seed embryos are believed to be useful in promoting sleep, blood circulation and virility. Traditionally, lotus seeds were sold only by Chinese medicinal shops because they were regarded more as a dried herb than a food. Today, more and more supermarkets are selling them prepacked and precooked to take the work out for you.

Preparing dried lotus seeds is time-consuming because removing the brown skin that clings to the seed is a fiddly task. Soak dried lotus seeds — 20 should suffice for one portion — in plenty of water for at least half an hour before rubbing off brown skins.

sweet treats

Some Chinese have the habit of preceding a meal with a sweet soup or drink, while others prefer to serve sweet, between-meal snacks. Sweet soups and drinks usually contain a marrow of some kind, watercress, lotus seeds, gingko nuts, dates and one of the milder Chinese herbs. It might seem a little confusing, too, why a distinction should exist between a sweet soup and a sweet drink when they appear so similar. There is only one explanation for this — tradition. The soups in question have always been served as part of a meal and the drinks outside mealtimes as sweet indulgence. As such, do not be overly bothered by the classifications herein. Suffice to know that rock sugar is the key ingredient in the following recipes.

Recipes

Lotus Seeds with Hard-boiled Eggs

COOKING TIME: 1 HOUR   SERVES 4–6

This is a 'cooling' brew that is often served as a pick-me-up, and the hard-boiled eggs give it extra substance.

Ingredients

Dried lotus seeds	200 g
Water	2 litres
Eggs	4–6
Rock sugar	200 g

Method

- Soak lotus seeds in plenty of water for 30 minutes or boil for 5 minutes. If boiled, allow seeds to cool before rubbing off brown skins if still attached. Split each lotus seed in two. Remove green core if still attached.
- Bring water to the boil. Add lotus seeds. Simmer for at least 45 minutes.
- Meanwhile, prepare hard-boiled eggs. To prevent eggs from cracking before they harden, immerse them in a pot of cold water and bring to the boil slowly. Simmer for 8 minutes, then remove to cool. Do not attempt to shell eggs when they are still hot as the shell will not come away cleanly.
- When lotus seeds are soft enough (taste one to test), add rock sugar and eggs. Heat for 5 minutes more to allow eggs to absorb liquid.

Cooking Know-how

Some brands of rock sugar come with a little grit, so you will need to strain the liquid after the rock sugar has melted for clarity. For added fragrance, tie two screwpine (*pandan*) leaves into a knot and add to the pot when simmering.

Time-saver

To avoid the hassle of preparing dried lotus seeds, substitute with 250 g precooked lotus seeds.

- Wash and drain precooked lotus seeds.
- Bring water to the boil. Add rock sugar. When sugar has completely dissolved, add lotus seeds. Simmer for 20 minutes or until lotus seeds are soft.
- Meanwhile, prepare hard-boiled eggs as advised.

Lotus Seeds and Solomon's Seal with Eggs

COOKING TIME: 45 MINUTES   SERVES 4

This recipe is a variation of the preceding one, with Solomon's seal added for aiding pancreatic functions and extra nourishment.

Ingredients

Precooked lotus seeds	200 g
Solomon's seal (*yu zhu/yok chok*)	15 g, rinsed
Rock sugar	150 g
Water	2 litres
Hard-boiled eggs	4, shelled

Method

- Except eggs, combine all other ingredients in a pot. Simmer for 40 minutes.
- Add shelled eggs in the last 5 minutes of simmering. Serve hot.

Cooking Know-how

If you want hard-boiled eggs that are well-shaped and have cooked yolks that are not askew, do not let eggs remain in one position as they cook. Instead, use a metal spoon to turn them around once or twice. This may be important to you if you plan to serve hard-boiled eggs cut up.

Opposite: Lotus Seeds with Hard-boiled Eggs.

Lotus Seeds and Chinese Yam

COOKING TIME: 45 MINUTES   SERVES 4

Lotus seeds are 'neutral' in energy and when combined with Chinese yam helps to regulate kidney functions.

Ingredients

Precooked lotus seeds	40, washed and drained
Chinese yam (*shan yao/wai san*)	20 g, rinsed
Rock sugar	150 g
Water	1.5 litres

Method

- Combine all ingredients in a pot. Simmer over low heat for 20 minutes.
- Strain if necessary. Reheat to serve warm. Refrigerate for 30 minutes to serve cold.

Lotus Seeds and Gingko Nuts

COOKING TIME: 45 MINUTES   SERVES 4

This is an ultra-simple and yet incredibly effective 'cooling' brew.

Ingredients

Water	2 litres
Dried gingko nuts	40–50, soaked in water for at least a few hours or preferably overnight
Precooked lotus seeds	250 g
Rock sugar	150 g

Method

- Bring water to the boil. Add gingko nuts. Simmer for 30 minutes.
- Add lotus seeds and rock sugar. Simmer for 15–20 minutes more, depending on the degree of softness you like for your lotus seeds and gingko nuts. Serve hot or cold.

Lotus Seeds and Gingko Nuts with Sterculia Seed

COOKING TIME: 1 HOUR   SERVES 4

Ingredients

Sterculia seed (*pang da hai/dai hau lam*)	1
Dried gingko nuts	40–50, soaked in water for at least a few hours or preferably overnight
Precooked lotus seeds	250 g
Water	2 litres
Rock sugar	150 g

Method

- Peel sterculia seed. Soak in plenty of cold water. Expansion begins after about 5 minutes. Remove all traces of peel and vein-like strands. Wash to remove fine grit. Set aside. Sterculia flesh does not need to be cooked.
- Bring gingko nuts, lotus seeds and water to the boil. Simmer over low heat for 20 minutes. When they are soft, add rock sugar. Simmer for 10–15 minutes more. When rock sugar has completely dissolved, remove from heat.
- Add as much sterculia flesh as required for each serving. Serve hot or cold.

Variations on a Five-flavoured Theme

The classic five-flavoured soup — barley, gingko nuts, lotus seeds, longan flesh and dried persimmon — is not an inflexible recipe. In fact, it varies slightly from dialect group to dialect group within the Chinese community, incorporating such ingredients as white tremella mushroom (bai mu er/shuet yi), more commonly known as white fungus; dried tangerine peel; sweet potatoes; agar-agar; red (adzuki) beans and even bird's nest. The list below draws together the key ingredients of the different versions of the five-flavoured soup. Exercise your culinary imagination and titillate the taste buds with permutations of not necessarily five, but two, three, four or even all of the listed ingredients, some of which are not herbs as such but are complementary to herbals blends.

Ingredients

Dried longan flesh	150 g
Dried persimmons	2, thinly sliced
Dried tangerine peel	6 pieces
Sweet potatoes	450 g
Agar-agar	60 g
Red (adzuki) beans	100 g
Bird's nest	30 g

Regardless of what you have chosen to include in your version of the five-flavoured soup, all recipes require a foundation of about 2 litres water, with 150–200 g rock sugar dissolved in it and either lotus seeds or gingko nuts for a basic ingredient. All recipes require an average of 45 minutes of simmering and serve 4–6 people. Find out how to process each of the listed ingredients below.

Dried longan flesh
Wash and remove all grit and impurities before adding to the pot in the last 15 minutes of simmering. Remember that dried longan flesh is already sweet, and thus, the amount of rock sugar otherwise called for by a recipe can be reduced by up to half, depending on your taste.

Dried persimmon
Fresh persimmons are round, fat, orange fruits with soft flesh and large pits. Dried persimmons, however, bear little resemblance to their fresh counterparts. Expect, instead, flattened brown discs, each covered with a thick dusting of white flour. To prepare dried persimmon, remove the hard centre, wash off the floury coating and cut into thin slices before adding to the pot in the last 15 minutes of simmering. It is slightly sweet, so cut down on rock sugar by about 60 g.

Dried tangerine peel
Simply add a few pieces in the last 15 minutes of simmering or at the beginning if you prefer a stronger citric presence. Be careful as too much will render your brew a little bitter.

Sweet potato
Peel and cut 1-cm thick slices. Add slices in the last 15 minutes of simmering Alternatively, cook slices separately with sugar, at a proportion of 450 g sweet potatoes to 150 g sugar in 1 litre water. If adopting the latter method, drain and dry a little before adding to the main pot in the last 5 minutes of simmering.

Agar-agar
Also referred to as Japanese gelatin, these translucent, raffia-like strands are made from seaweed and sold by most supermarkets. A fuss-free approach is to soak agar-agar for a few minutes, cut the softened strands into short lengths and then add to the pot in the last 2–3 minutes of cooking. Alternatively, boil about 700 ml water, add 30 g agar-agar strips and 100 g sugar, and cook for about 15 minutes until both are dissolved. Strain through a fine sieve and pour into a mould to set. When set, cut into fine shreds and add to individual bowls as required with other ingredients.

Red (adzuki) beans
Wash and boil about 100 g red beans for 30 minutes or until just cooked, but not mushy. Add to individual bowls as above.

Bird's nest
This ingredient increases the cooking time to at least 1 hour, and if it is being cooked directly from its dried state, it has to be added at the beginning together with such ingredients as gingko nuts or barley.

Gingko Nuts and Barley

COOKING TIME: 1 HOUR   SERVES 4

This 'cooling' brew is known to offset the detrimental effects of having eaten too many 'hot' foods. In TCM, gingko nuts are believed to strengthen the bladder and address related ailments. This was, in fact, the very reason that prompted my mother to cram handfuls of gingko nuts down my throat every week as a child. Today, some five decades later, I make it a point to eat gingko nuts whenever I feel the internal waterworks, as it were, not operating properly.

Ingredients

Dried gingko nuts	40–50, soaked in water for at least a few hours or preferably overnight
Barley	150 g
Water	2 litres
Screwpine (*pandan*) leaves (optional)	1–2, washed and tied into a knot
Rock sugar	150 g

Method

- Wash and drain soaked gingko nuts and barley. Bring washed ingredients and water to the boil. Simmer over medium heat for 20 minutes.
- Add screwpine leaves, if used, for added fragrance. Add rock sugar. Simmer for 40 minutes more.

Cooking Know-how

The state of gingko nuts — whether they are dried or have been soaked, and for how long — just before they are cooked affect the length of cooking time. When done, they should mash easily when pressed with the back of a spoon.

Green Beans and Rue with Tangerine Peel

COOKING TIME: 1 HOUR   SERVES 4

Ingredients

Water	2 litres
Green beans	250 g, thoroughly washed and drained
Rue (*chou cao/chow cho*)	10 g, washed and drained
Dried tangerine peel	3 pieces
Rock sugar	150 g

Method

- Bring water to the boil. Add green beans. Simmer for 30 minutes or until beans are just soft.
- Add rue and tangerine peel. Simmer for 15 minutes. By now, green beans should be very soft.
- Add rock sugar and simmer until dissolved. Serve hot or cold.

Opposite: Green Beans and Rue with Tangerine Peel.

Solomon's Seal with Chinese Almonds

COOKING TIME: 1 HOUR   SERVES 4

Chinese almonds (xing ren/hung ngan) are really apricot kernels, and there are two types: sweet and bitter. Both types look much alike, except that the bitter ones are smaller and rounder. The bitter kernels are also rarely used without their sweet counterparts. Combining the two not only acts to 'cool' the body, but also makes a powerful expectorant. Apricot kernels in general are trusted remedies for dry coughs, laryngitis and respiratory ailments.

Ingredients

Solomon's seal (*yu zhu/yok chok*)	15 g, rinsed and drained
Sweet apricot kernels (*nan xing/nam hung*)	40, rinsed and drained
Bitter apricot kernels (*bei xing/puk hung*)	40, rinsed and drained
Water	2 litres
Rock sugar	150 g

Method

- Except rock sugar, combine all other ingredients in a pot. Bring to the boil. Simmer over low heat for 40 minutes.
- Add rock sugar. Simmer for 15 minutes more. Serve warm.

Solomon's Seal with Apricot Kernels and Lotus Seeds

COOKING TIME: 1 HOUR   SERVES 4

These three ingredients combine particularly well for a subtle flavour.

Ingredients

Solomon's seal (*yu zhu/yok chok*)	15 g, rinsed
Sweet apricot kernels (*nan xing/nam hung*)	40, rinsed
Water	2 litres
Rock sugar	150 g
Precooked lotus seeds	200 g

Method

- Bring rinsed ingredients and water to the boil. Simmer for 30 minutes.
- Add rock sugar. Simmer over medium heat for 10 minutes more.
- Add lotus seeds. Simmer for 15 minutes or until soft. Serve hot or cold.

Opposite: Solomon's Seal with Chinese Almonds.

sweet soups

Among sweet brews that I have learnt to love are those that simmer vegetable marrows long and lovingly with one herb or another and some rock sugar. I did not take kindly to them initially because I had always associated vegetable marrows with savoury dishes. Nevertheless, once I got used to the sweetish flavour of these drinks, which are really more like soups because of their hearty nature, I was forever enamoured.

The Cantonese are particularly fond of using the brown marrow, which they call *lo wong kwa*, or "old cucumber", and watercress for sweet soups, both of which are reputedly good for dry coughs. The soups are usually served hot but may be served chilled if you so fancy. Do be mindful that red dates impart a considerable amount of sweetness, so rock sugar can be either avoided altogether or reduced to taste.

Recipes

herbal drinks

You might well ask what the difference is between a sweet herbal soup and a sweet herbal drink. The line of distinction would be that of substance, with the former being heartier and correspondingly heavier, while the latter is lighter and more of a thirst-quencher.

Recipes

Codonopsis Root and Chrysanthemum

COOKING TIME: 45 MINUTES   SERVES 4

Although codonopsis root (dang shen/dong sum) is not strictly of the ginseng family, it can be used for similar purposes — as a 'warming' tonic. People who suffer from high blood pressure, however, are generally advised to avoid ginseng and codonopsis, too, comes under this category, although it is significantly less 'hot' than ginseng.

Ingredients

Codonopsis root (*dang shen/dong sum*)	30 g, rinsed
Dried chrysanthemum petals	15 g
Rock sugar	150 g
Water	1 litre

Method

- Combine all ingredients in a pot. Simmer over low heat for at least 45 minutes.
- Either strain off pulp or allow to settle before drinking.

Bird's Nest Drink

COOKING TIME: 1–2 HOURS   SERVES 2–4

Bird's nest is not strictly a medicinal herb but enjoys a good reputation for being a 'warming' food that helps ward off colds and flu-related ailments. Although bird's nest should really be found in the category of double-boiled dishes, it has been included here because bird's nest can also be simmered slowly with rock sugar to make a refreshing drink. There are as many grades of bird's nest as there are feathers on the bird, so the richness of your bird's nest drink essentially depends on the depth of your pocket. For this recipe, the amount of rock sugar can be increased or decreased according to taste.

Ingredients

Bird's nest	60 g
Rock sugar	150 g
Screwpine (*pandan*) leaves	2
Water	1 litre

Method

- Combine all ingredients in a heavy-bottomed or good enamel pot. Simmer for 1–2 hours. The pot should have a snug-fitting lid to prevent excessive evaporation.
- Check liquid level occasionally. Add a little water if necessary. Serve warm or thoroughly chilled.

Cooking Know-how

Most herbalists sell bird's nest that is already cleaned. Cleaning unprocessed bird's nest can be tedious and time-consuming. To prepare bird's nest that is in its natural state, first use a pair of previously unused or suitably clean tweezers to pick out impurities like tiny twigs and feathers, then wash several times. The last change of water should be spotlessly clean.

Opposite: Bird's Nest Drink.

herbal teas

Basic Chinese tea is said to reduce excess 'heat' in the body, quench thirst and soothe minor discomforts or irritations. Depending on the concoction, herbal teas can help clear lungs, dissipate heatiness, kill bacteria, boost immunity, lower blood sugar, reduce phlegm and detoxify.

Recipes

savoury stews

If there is one category of herbal cooking I enjoy dwelling at length upon, it is this one — the savoury herbal stew. Over centuries, recipes in this category have earned the reputation of being delicious, nourishing and extremely 'warming'. In order to appreciate them, one has to first understand the importance of liquid sustenance to the Chinese psyche. It is, to some extent, a throwback to rather more impoverished times when food was scarce and only the most watery gruel provided daily sustenance. Soups were created for their all-in-one ability to provide sustenance. Fuel, too, was scarce and cooking the family meal over one precious fire was a better option than flaring several clay ovens. Thus, soups have become an integral part of the Chinese meal, entirely different from their western counterpart. While the latter are meant to be appetisers, the former are borne with pride to the table to sit amid other dishes and be sipped ever so appreciatively through the meal. In fact, in days gone by, no Chinese meal would have been regarded as complete if it did not consist of "four plates and a bowl", alluding to four dishes, which may be stir-fried, braised or steamed, and the central bowl of hot, steaming soup.

Herbal soups rarely have a strong medicinal taste or bitterness characteristic of other medicinal herbs not usually used in daily cooking. It is also a fallacy that cooking these dishes is troublesome. Rather, the reverse is true once you have learnt the basic principles of herbal preparation: that the blend is all-important and that there are only three methods — slow cooking or simmering, steaming and double-boiling. Moreover, modern science has since contributed the pressure cooker, which should be viewed as a convenient and time-saving device rather than a culinary sell-out. All of the herbalists I have since spoken to dismissed the theory that pressure cooking is not acceptable because it diminishes nutritional value. Pressure cooking, in fact, traps in more nutrients by ensuring practically no evaporation. Tradition dies hard, nevertheless, and many elderly Chinese will still insist on simmering, maybe even over charcoal embers.

Recipes

Chicken or Lean Pork with Ginseng Shreds

COOKING TIME: 1 HOUR   SERVES 4

The ginseng called for in this recipe is not the root itself, but the thin, stringy roots that extend from the main stalk. The Cantonese call these shreds yong sam soe, *which literally means the "beard of the ginseng root". The beard, as it were, is a mild form of the potent root and makes a good introduction for those who are consuming it for the first time. It is extremely palatable, with only a slight bitter taste and is good for restoring the body's 'heat'.*

Ingredients

Chicken	1, about 1 kg, or 600 g lean pork
Ginseng shreds	30 g
Water	1 litre
Salt	2 tsp

Method

- Clean chicken thoroughly. Remove head and feet, as well as skin if desired. If using pork, wash and leave in one piece.
- Except salt, combine all other ingredients in a pot. Cover and bring to the boil. Simmer over low heat for about 1 hour. Add salt in the last few minutes of cooking.

Cooking Know-how

Although tradition often decrees that a whole bird is used, there is no reason why it cannot be substituted with chicken joints as there is no difference in flavour.

Chicken with Cordyceps and Chinese Yam

COOKING TIME: 1 HOUR 30 MINUTES   SERVES 4

Ingredients

Chicken	1, about 900 g
Cordyceps (*dong chong xia cao/tung chung cho*)	30 g, rinsed
Chinese yam (*shan yao/wai san*)	15 g, rinsed
Water	1.5 litres
Salt	2 tsp

Method

- Combine all ingredients in a pot. Simmer over very low heat for at least 1 hour 30 minutes. Before serving, skim off as much fat as possible.

Chicken or Lean Pork with White Fungus

COOKING TIME: 40 MINUTES   SERVES 4

Ingredients

Chicken	1, about 1 kg, or 400 g lean pork
White fungus (*bai mu er/shuet yi*)	30 g
Water	1 litre
Salt	2 tsp

Method

- Clean chicken thoroughly, and skin if desired. If using pork, trim off any fat if desired, but leave in one piece or cut into two large chunks.
- Soak white fungus in warm water. Remove all impurities. Wash and drain slightly expanded fungus, squeezing out all moisture.
- Except white fungus, combine all other ingredients in a pot. Simmer for 20 minutes. Add white fungus. Simmer for 20 minutes more.

Opposite: Chicken or Lean Pork with White Fungus.

Pork with Eucommia Bark and Chinese Angelica

COOKING TIME: 1 HOUR   SERVES 4

Eucommia bark reputedly detoxifies and is effective in the treatment of lumbago and muscular weakness. Chicken or mutton can be used in place of lean pork in this recipe.

Ingredients

Lean pork	750 g, washed, trimmed of excess fat and cut into large chunks
Eucommia bark (*du zhong/dou chong*)	8 g, rinsed
Chinese angelica (*dang gui/dong kwai*)	8 g, rinsed
Dried red dates (*hong zao/hung cho*)	10, pitted and rinsed
Salt	2 tsp
Carrot	1, cut into large chunks

Method

- Except carrot, combine all other ingredients in a pot. Bring to the boil. Simmer over lower heat for 45 minutes.
- Add carrots. Simmer for 15 minutes more. Discard herbs, then serve hot.

Pork with Falsestarwort and Lilyturf Roots, Apricot Kernels and Pears

COOKING TIME: 1 HOUR   SERVES 4

Both pears and lilyturf root are famous 'coolants' and this unusual blend is said to help alleviate dry coughs, moisten the lungs, balance Qi and promote Yin properties.

Ingredients

Lean pork	450 g
Falsestarwort root (*tai zi sheng/tai chi sam*)	15 g, washed and drained
Lilyturf root (*mai dong/mak tung*)	15 g, washed and drained
Bitter apricot kernels (*bei xing/puk hung*)	20, washed and drained
Sweet apricot kernels (*nan xing/nam hung*)	20, washed and drained
Pears	4, peeled, cored and quartered
Salt	2 tsp
Water	1 litre

Method

- Combine all ingredients in a pot. Simmer for about 1 hour.

Cooking know-how

If you want to retain some of the bite in the pears, add them only in the last 30 minutes of cooking.

Opposite: Pork with Falsestarwort and Lilyturf Roots, Apricot Kernels and Pears.

Pork with Skullcap, Solomon's Seal, Lotus Seeds and Barley

COOKING TIME: 2 HOURS   SERVES 4

The full name of skullcap is barbat skullcap scutellaria, or ban zhi lian in Mandarin, and its botanical name is scutellaria barbata herba. Skullcap, when combined with the other herbs in this recipe, promotes good Qi and healthy spleen and stomach functions.

Ingredients

Dried lotus seeds	2 Tbsp
Barley	2 Tbsp
Skullcap	5 g, rinsed and drained
Solomon's seal (yu zhu/yok chok)	10 g, rinsed and drained
Lean pork	450 g
Water	1 litre
Salt	2 tsp

Method

- Soak lotus seeds and barley for a few hours before cooking. Alternatively, separately boil them for 30 minutes. Precooked lotus seeds can be substituted to save some time.
- Combine all ingredients in a pot. Cover and bring to the boil. Simmer over medium heat for 1–2 hours.

Duck with Lotus Seeds, Barley and Tangerine Peel

COOKING TIME: 2 HOURS   SERVES 4

This may sound like an unlikely combination but the result is positively ambrosial if you like duck. This rich fowl is rarely given a chance to vindicate itself and most will simply turn up their noses on account of the duck's undeserved reputation for having a strong odour. Well-prepared duck has only the faintest odour and with the guilty glands removed from the region of the parson's nose, it can be the most beautiful bird. Remember, too, that duck is extremely fatty and unless you like a layer of duck fat floating on the surface of your soup, remove the skin.

Ingredients

Duck	1, about 1.5 kg
Barley	100 g, washed and drained
Dried tangerine peel	5 pieces
Water	2 litres
Salt	2 tsp
Ground white pepper (optional)	1 tsp
Precooked lotus seeds	40, washed and drained

Method

- Clean duck thoroughly. Cut off and discard head and feet, unless you have a passion for them. Cut remaining duck into 8 joints. Remove every shred of blood and entrails. Skin if desired Wash with plenty of salt. Drain well.
- Except lotus seeds, combine all other ingredients in a pot. Cover and simmer for 2 hours. Check liquid level occasionally. Add lotus seeds in the last 20 minutes of simmering.

Time-saver

This recipe can be prepared with a pressure cooker. Halve the amount of water to 1 litre, simmer over medium heat for 45 minutes, then remove from heat. Add lotus seeds to cook, uncovered and without pressure. Simmer for 20 minutes. If soup is oily, allow to cool and remove layer of duck fat with a spoon.

Opposite: Duck with Lotus Seeds, Barley and Tangerine Peel.

Chicken with Korean Ginseng

COOKING TIME: 1 HOUR   SERVES 4

There are those who will gladly part with a great deal of money for a root of premium ginseng with the belief that it is a magical elixir. Korean ginseng (gao li shen/go lai sam) is quite similar to Chinese ginseng but is regarded by some as being more potent. At some food exhibitions where superior ginseng is kept under lock and key, Korean ginseng has been known to cost tens of thousands of dollars. This is not a soup to be sipped amid anything less than tranquil ambience. Like approaching the best wine, the state of mind brooks no distraction. Above all, the palate must be receptive to this herby nectar. If nothing else, you have spent a great deal of money for a few moments of pure culinary pleasure.

Ingredients

Chicken	1, about 900 g
Korean ginseng	60 g
Water	1 litre
Salt	2 tsp

Method

- Clean chicken thoroughly. Remove head, feet and/or skin as desired.
- Combine all ingredients in a pot. Simmer for about 1 hour.
- When you are satisfied with the taste and consistency of your precious soup, you absolutely must serve it in the finest porcelain.

Chicken with Ginseng and Foxglove Root

COOKING TIME 1 HOUR   SERVES 4

Every now and then, herbalists will mention an uncertain category of ginseng (pao shen/pao sam) with no classifying name in English. While some herbalists define pao shen as American ginseng or a species of ginseng, others identify it more as a grade of ginseng, and a superior one at that. Where there is no confusion about pao shen, however, is its price. Pao shen is usually more expensive. Ask your herbalist to recommend what is best suited to this recipe. Foxglove root is prescribed by herbalists for the treatment of coughs, headaches, vertigo and low blood pressure, as well as for disorders of the kidney and lungs.

Ingredients

Chicken	1, about 1.5 kg
Ginseng (*pao shen/ pau sam*)	20 g , rinsed and drained
Foxglove root (*shou di huang/sok tei*)	20 g, rinsed and drained
Water	1 litre
Salt	2 tsp

Method

- Combine all ingredients in a pot. Cover and simmer for 1 hour. Serve hot.
- The resulting chicken meat would be relatively tasteless, but there is no sense in wasting it. Eat with a side dip of dark soy sauce.

Opposite: Chicken with Korean Ginseng.

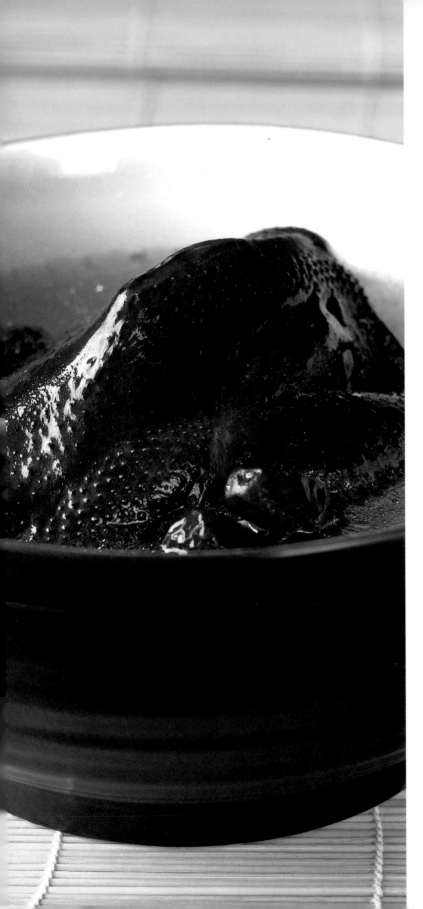

Black Chicken and Ginseng

COOKING TIME: 1 HOUR SERVES 4

Black chickens are generally smaller than their ordinary counterparts and have, for centuries, been deemed superior because of their said restorative properties. Colour and size aside, black chickens are no different in taste and texture. This recipe also does not require a specific type of ginseng and what you eventually put in the pot really depends on what you have selected at the shop.

Ingredients

Black chicken	1, about 650 g
Ginseng	15 g, rinsed and drained
Chinese angelica (*dang gui/dong kwai*)	30 g, rinsed and drained
Dried red dates (*hong zao/hung cho*)	10, pitted, rinsed and drained
Water	1 litre
Salt	2 tsp

Method

- Clean chicken thoroughly. Leave whole or cut into 4 large joints if preferred.
- Combine all ingredients in a pot. Bring to the boil. Simmer over lower heat for 45 minutes or until chicken is tender.
- Except dates, discard all herbs. Serve warm.

Chicken with Bird's Nest and Ginseng

COOKING TIME: 1 HOUR   SERVES 4

This is a herbier version of the previous recipe with the addition of ginseng. The tradition is also to use the best ginseng you can afford for economy has no place in the pursuit of good, nourishing Chinese soups.

Ingredients

Chicken	1, about 900 g
Bird's nest	200 g, soaked and thoroughly cleaned
Ginseng	60 g
Water	1 litre
Salt	2 tsp

Method

- Clean chicken thoroughly. Skin if desired.
- Combine all ingredients in a pot. Simmer for at least 1 hour.

Cooking Know-how

The longer bird's nest is soaked prior to cooking, the softer it becomes. For this recipe, however, soaking the bird's nest for ages before cooking does not count for much because it is simmered for a prolonged period of time anyway.

Chicken or Lean Pork with Bird's Nest

COOKING TIME: 1 HOUR   SERVES 4

This is where bird's nest really shines — as a star ingredient in a savoury soup that is rich with all the natural goodness of chicken or lean pork. Perhaps more than any other combination, bird's nest and white meat in a lightly fragrant soup make not only warming sustenance, but also a classic palate refresher. It is for this reason that a light soup is sometimes served near the end of a multiple-course Chinese meal — to clean the palate after heavy dishes in preparation for what is yet to come.

Ingredients

Chicken	1, about 900 g, or 400 g lean pork
Bird's nest	90 g, soaked and thoroughly cleaned
Water	1 litre
Salt	2 tsp

Method

- Combine all ingredients in a pot. Simmer for 1 hour. Serve hot. Add a sprinkling of good, white pepper if desired.
- If you are serving the family individual bowls of soup, it is as well to shred the chicken after removing all traces of skin and fat.

Chicken or Lean Pork with Solomon's Seal

COOKING TIME: 1 HOUR–1 HOUR 30 MINUTES   SERVES 4

This is a clear soup made from either chicken or lean pork, depending on your preference. As chicken comes with a percentage of inedible bones and gristle, the amount specified is always more than that for pork. It is entirely optional whether the chicken is skinned or not, and likewise whether it is left whole or cut up. If using pork, it should be cut into large chunks, if at all, and not thin slices. While this is more a tradition than an instruction in pursuit of better nutritional results, a herbal soup somehow does not look right with thin slices of meat floating about.

Ingredients

Chicken	1, about 900 g, or 600 g lean pork
Solomon's seal (*yu zhu/yok chok*)	15 g, rinsed and drained
Water	1 litre
Salt	2 tsp

Method

- Clean chicken thoroughly. Remove head and feet. If using pork, wash and leave in one piece.
- Combine all ingredients in a pot. Simmer for between 1 hour and 1 hour 30 minutes, depending on heat intensity. Adjust to taste if necessary. Drink soup warm.

Chicken or Lean Pork with Solomon's Seal and Chinese Yam

COOKING TIME: 1 HOUR   SERVES 4

When herbalists prescribe pork with a given blend, they will always recommend that you use the leanest cut possible. Pork fat may have little nutritional value, but the tiniest bit of fat renders any soup more flavourful and "smooth", as the Cantonese have come to describe with the term wat. *Anything that is* wat *has a texture akin to that of butter-smoothness. In this recipe, however, the soup is drunk for nourishment and so the smoothness or* wat *factor is not as important.*

Ingredients

Chicken	1, about 1 kg, or 600 g lean pork
Solomon's seal (*yu zhu/yok chok*)	15 g, rinsed
Chinese yam (*shan yao/wai san*)	15 g, rinsed
Water	1 litre
Salt	2 tsp

Method

- Clean chicken thoroughly. Remove excess fatty skin. Leave whole. If using pork, trim off any fat if desired, but leave in one piece.
- Combine all ingredients in a pot. Simmer for about 1 hour.

Cooking Know-how

A certain amount of evaporation is expected with any slow simmering process, especially if the pot used does not have a snug-fitting lid. Evaporation, however, also means a reduction of liquid and consequently a concentration of flavour. Expect about 20 per cent of reduction for every hour of simmering, although a lot depends on heat intensity and size of pot. As long as the final yield is about 4 medium-sized bowls, each about 500 ml, the proportion of water is correct.

Chicken or Lean Pork and Ginseng's Top

COOKING TIME: 45 MINUTES   SERVES 4

The ginseng called for in this recipe is neither the main stalk nor the shreds, but the top and thicker end of the main stalk called yong sam tau *by the Cantonese and means the "head of the ginseng root". The 'head' of the ginseng is stronger in flavour than the 'beard' and is also said to possess more Yang energy. Although this recipe says to use either chicken or pork, a combination of half and half is also plausible.*

Ingredients

Spring chicken	1, about 400 g, or 400 g lean pork
Ginseng's top	30 g
Water	1 litre
Salt	2 tsp

Method

- Clean chicken thoroughly. Remove head and feet. It is unnecessary to skin a spring chicken as it is already lean. If using pork, wash and leave in one piece.
- Combine all ingredients in a pot. Simmer for 45 minutes.

Cooking Know-how

A spring chicken does not need much more than 45 minutes of simmering to have most of its flavour and goodness extracted. It is useful to remember here that the true test of herbal soups lies not in how tender the meat is but how flavourful the soup has become.

Chicken or Lean Pork with Solomon's Seal, Chinese Yam and Wolfberries

COOKING TIME: 1 HOUR   SERVES 4

Chinese wolfberries are reputedly good for the eyes and have a delicately sweet flavour. Children are often given a few of them to munch straight off the medicinal shop counter, but they are best simmered with poultry or robust meats like lamb or mutton. As a rough guide, use a handful or about 2 Tbsp for every 4 serves of soup.

Ingredients

Chicken	1, about 900 g, or 600 g lean pork
Solomon's seal (*yu zhu/yok chok*)	15 g, rinsed
Chinese yam (*shan yao/wai san*)	15 g, rinsed
Chinese wolfberries (*gou qi zi/gei chi*)	2 Tbsp, rinsed
Water	1.5 litres
Salt	2 tsp

Method

- Clean chicken thoroughly. Remove excess fatty skin. Either leave whole or cut into large joints. If using pork, cut into bite-sized chunks.
- Combine all ingredients in a pot. Simmer for about 1 hour.
- Garnish with a sprinkling of ground white pepper and fresh coriander (cilantro) leaves, also known as Chinese parsley.

Cooking Know-how

If you are making this dish in advance, allow to cool completely before skimming off fat from the surface for a less oily dish. If guests are involved, try serving the soup in shim bowls with lids for what seems to me to be the epitome of civilised dining.

Chicken and Chinese Angelica

COOKING TIME: 1 HOUR   SERVES 4

Chinese angelica is usually prescribed for gynaecological disorders but there is absolutely no reason why non-sufferers cannot enjoy it. For new mothers with a bout of those post-natal blues, try nursing them with some of this chicken soup. Discard not a single shred of chicken except gristle and bone, and down the soup to the last drop.

Ingredients

Chicken	1, about 1.5 kg
Chinese angelica (*dang gui/dong kwai*)	30 g, rinsed
Water	1.5 litres
Salt	2 tsp

Method

- Clean chicken thoroughly. Leave skin on and whole.
- Combine all ingredients in a pot. Simmer for about 1 hour.

Duck with Winter Melon, Gingko Nuts and Tangerine Peel

COOKING TIME: 1 HOUR 30 MINUTES   SERVES 4

The combined balance of a strong-flavoured meat like duck, delicate winter melon, a hint of tangerine and the mildly bitter gingko nuts is particularly captivating.

Ingredients

Duck	1, about 2 kg
Winter melon	1, about 450 g
Dried tangerine peel	4–5 pieces
Water	2 litres
Salt	2 tsp
Precooked gingko nuts	40, washed and drained

Method

- Clean duck thoroughly. Remove head and feet. Cut into 8 large joints.
- Peel winter melon, then halve. Remove soft centre and seeds. Cut remaining flesh into large chunks. Wash and drain.
- Except gingko nuts and winter melon, combine all other ingredients in a pot. Simmer for about 1 hour. Add remaining ingredients. Simmer for 30 minutes more.

Time-saver

If using a pressure cooker, halve the specified amount of water to 1 litre. Except winter melon chunks and precooked gingko nuts, combine all other ingredients and pressure cook for 30 minutes. Add remaining ingredients. Pressure cook for 15 minutes more. If using dried gingko nuts, they should be soaked for several hours and then added for the entire pressure cooking time.

Pig's Heart with Lotus Seeds, Longan and Falsestarwort Root

COOKING TIME: 1 HOUR   SERVES 4

Whatever your feelings about the animal's organ, this recipe helps calm nerves and reduces palpitations and insomnia.

Ingredients

Pig's heart	1, about 300 g
Dried lotus seeds	20 g
Falsestarwort root (*tai zi sheng/tai chi sam*)	10 g, washed and drained
Dried longan flesh	10 g, washed and drained
Water	1 litre
Salt	2 tsp

Method

- Wash pig's heart. Trim off tendons and remove traces of blood. Leave whole or cut into two large pieces.
- Boil lotus seeds for 30 minutes. Drain. Alternatively, precooked lotus seeds can be substituted to save some time.
- Combine all ingredients in a pot. Simmer for 1 hour.

Chicken Feet with Peanuts, Red Beans and Tangerine Peel

COOKING TIME: 2–3 HOURS   SERVES 4

Those unaccustomed might assume chicken feet here refer to the meaty thighs or legs. They do not. Chicken feet in this recipe are the scaly, bony lower limbs, claws included. They also happen to be delicious if treated right. It is no more uncivilized eating them than salivating over blue cheese. Never mind that chicken feet are extraordinarily cheap and usually ignored, they can still be coaxed to part with substantial nutrition and flavour. Besides, there is as much nutrition in the peanuts and red beans as there is flavour in the dried tangerine peel. Some Chinese believe that children given a steady diet of this dish will develop strong muscles.

Ingredients

Chicken feet	20–30
Shelled raw peanuts (groundnuts)	250 g
Red (adzuki) beans	100 g, washed and drained
Dried tangerine peel	4–5 pieces
Water	2 litres
Salt	3 tsp

Method

- Remove scaly outer skin of chicken feet. Cut off sharp talons. Wash in several changes of water. Drain.
- Boil peanuts for a few minutes. Allow to cool before rubbing off skins if necessary.
- Combine all ingredients in a pot. Simmer for 2–3 hours.

Cooking Know-how

If you are disinclined to prepare so many ingredients, simply combine chicken feet and peanuts in a pressure cooker for about 1 hour for a quick-and-easy soup.

double-boiled
dishes

Although this is not a method of cooking that endears itself to anyone living in the fast lane of life, it is one that has transcended all social and economic barriers through centuries of Chinese culinary history. Although some may regard the whole business of cooking as a tedious chore if it deviates even slightly from microwave heating, it is really their loss for not finding the true joy of good food cooked with tender loving care.

Double-boiling is a technique that involves placing food in a container that sits suspended inside another, larger container. The latter of which contains a modest amount of boiling water and is what sits over the flame or source of heat. As such, the food has no direct contact with heat, and steam from the boiling water is all that powers the gentle simmering characteristic of double-boiled cooking. Food in a double-boiler does not so much boil as bubble and shudder over a long period of time. There is also no chance of burning and evaporation is minimal, so most nutrients are really sealed in provided the smaller container has a snug-fitting lid. Unlike the relatively makeshift *bain-marie*, the French method of cooking over boiling water European cooks employ for delicate custards and junkets to prevent burning and curdling, little steam escapes from the sides of a double-boiler.

There are several fundamental rules in double-boiling. First, water in the larger container should never be at a level that will force the smaller container upward like a driven piston when it boils; this simply means that too much water was added. Second, always have on standby boiling or at least hot water to add to the larger, outer container when needed so the cooking temperature does not drop suddenly as it would if you had added cold water. Third, double-boilers should only be placed over low to medium heat.

Just about every stew, soup, gruel or liquid-based dish may be double-boiled with pleasing results. It is particularly good for food that tends to break up with prolonged simmering.

Recipes

Pork with Figs and Falsestarwort Root

COOKING TIME: 1 HOUR   SERVES 4

This double-boiled dish from Dr. Geng helps to promote Qi, strengthens the immunity system and blood function and improves the digestive process.

Ingredients

Lean pork	250 g, sliced into thick pieces
Fresh figs	4, stems removed and left whole
Falsestarwort root (*tai zi shen/tai chi sam*)	20 g, washed and drained
Salt	2 tsp
Water	750 ml

Method

- Combine all ingredients in a double-boiler. Simmer for 1 hour or until pork is very tender.

Cooking know-how

Dried figs, if available, can also be used for this dish. Note, however, that some vendors sell them sugared.

Bird's Nest and Chicken

COOKING TIME: 2 HOURS   SERVES 4

Of all the double-boiled dishes, this one is perhaps the most frequently cooked. With only bird's nest and chicken as ingredients, there is not the slightest hint of herbal flavour, appeasing people who might find even the mildest herb off-putting. It is basically a light, refreshing soup that can be drunk at any time of the day.

Ingredients

Chicken	1, about 900 g
Bird's nest	60 g, washed and thoroughly cleaned
Water	1 litre
Salt	2 tsp

Method

- Clean chicken thoroughly. Remove head and feet, as well as skin if desired.
- Combine all ingredients in a double-boiler. Simmer for 2 hours.

Cooking Know-how

It does not make one jot of difference to the nourishment of the dish if you do include gizzard in this recipe. The presence of gizzard only darkens the soup.

Opposite: Pork with Figs and Falsestarwort Root.

Chicken, Bird's Nest and Ginseng

COOKING TIME: 2 HOURS   SERVES 4

This is an all-time favourite of mine even if it does cost a pretty penny. On lean days, I buy loose pieces of bird's nest for a few dollars, use a mere hint of ginseng and splurge on the chicken. After all, how much can a chicken cost? Nevertheless, it is the chicken that I tear into after consuming the soup even though it is relatively tasteless. My mother used to make a decent dish of the double-boiled chicken. She would cut the drained chicken into large joints, and then deep-fry them after marinating them in dark soy sauce.

Ingredients

Chicken	1, about 900 g
Bird's nest	60 g, washed and thoroughly cleaned
Ginseng	15 g
Water	1 litre
Salt	2 tsp

Method

- Skin and clean chicken thoroughly. When bird's nest is also part of the recipe, the chicken used should be as lean as possible because the resulting soup should be clear and light for the flavour of the bird's nest to come through.
- Combine all ingredients in a double-boiler. Simmer for 2 hours.

Duck with Cordyceps, Foxglove Root and Red Dates

COOKING TIME: 2 HOURS   SERVES 6

Cordyceps and foxglove root together help to strengthen kidney function and the lungs. The mighty combination is also said to alleviate coughs and night sweats.

Ingredients

Duck	1, cleaned and trimmed
Cordyceps (*dong chong xia cao/tung chung cho*)	5 g, washed and drained
Dried red dates (*hong zao/hung cho*)	10, washed and drained
Foxglove root (*shou di huang/sok dei*)	15 g
Salt	2 tsp
Water	1 litre

Method

- Combine all ingredients in a double-boiler. Simmer for at least 2 hours or until duck is fork tender.

Cooking Know-how

If you can find French-cut duck breasts, substitute whole duck with 700 g duck breast for a much less oily dish. Skinned, the duck breasts consist of mostly lean meat.

White Fungus and Chicken

COOKING TIME: 1 HOUR 30 MINUTES   SERVES 4

For want of a better description, this dish is a watered-down version of bird's nest and chicken. Nevertheless, it is a delicious soup with crunch from the white fungus that bird's nest does not have.

Ingredients

Chicken	1, about 900 g
White fungus	
(*bai mu er/shuet yi*)	100 g, soaked and thoroughly cleaned
Water	1 litre
Salt	2 tsp
Light soy sauce	1 tsp
Ground white pepper	1 tsp
Fresh coriander (cilantro) leaves	

Method

- Clean chicken thoroughly. Remove head and feet if desired, but do not skin. This soup is tastier with a little fat in it.
- Combine chicken, white fungus, water and salt in a double-boiler. Simmer for 1 hour 30 minutes. Serve hot with light soy sauce, pepper and coriander.

Cooking Know-how

Pieces of white fungus are pale yellow and each have a hard bit attached. Snip this off before soaking. Also, if after soaking you find that you have a little more than you need, keep the excess in a covered container for use another day.

Notoginseng Root and Chicken

COOKING TIME: 2 HOURS   SERVES 4

Notoginseng root looks like a stone and rather unappealing at first sight, but it has been brewed for centuries for specific ailments like internal bruising and, if you would so believe, a diminished male libido! My first personal experience with notoginseng occurred some years ago after a small army-training accident. I had fallen into a U-boat and bashed myself in a few places that rendered me so sore that I was somewhat immobile for a month. When I came home from hospital, I was advised to drink this brew for a week. Certainly, I recovered.

Method

- Except light soy sauce and pepper, combine all other ingredients in a double-boiler. Simmer for 2 hours.
- The addition of soy sauce before serving is a personal habit as I rather prefer the rich saltiness of this ingredient to plain salt. Also, pepper gives any savoury soup a kick and helps it go down, especially when you are not particularly fond of strong herbs.

Ingredients

Chicken	1, about 900 g
Notoginseng root	
(*tian qi/teen chat*)	30 g
Water	1 litre
Salt	2 tsp
Light soy sauce	1 tsp
Ground white pepper	1 tsp

Spare Ribs with Chinese Yam, Angelica and Wolfberries

COOKING TIME: 2 HOURS; SERVES 2

Chinese yam aids the lungs and kidneys and generally nourishes the whole body. All cuts of pork, including spare ribs, are deemed 'neutral' and could become Yin or Yang in energy, depending on the herbs used. This is a 'warming' or Yang dish and is especially good for women after giving birth.

Ingredients

Pork spare ribs	500 g, cut into large pieces and excess fat trimmed
Chinese yam (*shan yao/wai san*)	8 g, rinsed and drained
Chinese angelica (*dang gui/dong kwai*)	8 g, rinsed and drained
Chinese wolfberries (*gou qi zi/gei chi*)	2 Tbsp, rinsed and drained
Water	1 litre
Salt	2 tsp

Method

• Combine all ingredients in a double-boiler. Cook over medium heat for 2 hours. Discard herbs. Serve with rice.

Cooking Know-how

This recipe can also be prepared through conventional stove-top cooking, gas or electric. In a covered pot, simmer over medium heat for about 1 hour.

herbal one -
pot meals

This category encompasses a range of dishes cooked frequently at home and in some restaurants. Most of these dishes are rich and complex experiences, and a number are also expensive to prepare by virtue of the cost of such ingredients as dried scallops, abalone and quality Chinese mushrooms.

Cooking these dishes at home should present little trouble once you understand the principles of slow cooking, the characteristics of each ingredient and the concepts of balancing and blending flavours. There is also much less mystique in these dishes as they are eaten more for their taste than their curative properties. Within the range of recipes lie many possibilities to create new and interesting dishes as guided by your preferences in taste and texture. For instance, lotus root is known to go well with pork spare ribs, but you may well wish to try combining it with chestnuts and pig's tripe instead. Unorthodox perhaps, but not to say it cannot be nutritious and tasty.

The most arresting feature of these dishes is that the amounts of ingredients specified are not derived from an exacting science. Whether you use 20 chestnuts with one chicken or 40 chestnuts with half a chicken makes little difference to the ultimate enjoyment of the dish. It is only a question of striking a perfect balance of flavours and textures for youself, finding the personal formula that pleases. These are also the dishes you can cook and present with great pride and flourish when you want to entertain special guests. They are elegant and say much for a cook's flair for delicate composition.

Recipes

Stuffed Pigeon with Chestnuts and Lotus Seeds

COOKING TIME: 45 MINUTES   SERVES 4

Dismiss the notion that a fat, cooing pigeon is an adorable living creature and you will be able to eat this dish without the slightest bit of queasiness. Deep-fried pigeons have been a banquet delicacy for as long as I can remember, and provided I do not have to kill the birds myself, I would eat them with gusto. Do not believe the old wives' tale that the only way to kill pigeons is by suffocating them. Instead, buy prepared pigeons from supermarkets. Humane sentiments aside, pigeon meat is sweeter and more tender than chicken.

Ingredients

Pigeons	2, total weight about 600 g
Dried chestnuts	40, boiled for 15 minutes and with skins rubbed off when cooled, then washed and drained
Precooked lotus seeds	40, washed and drained
Salt	2 tsp
Ground black pepper	1/2 tsp
Water	1 litre

Method

- Clean pigeons thoroughly. Remove heads and feet. Wash and drain.
- Except water, combine all other ingredients. Stuff mixture into pigeons.
- Place pigeons in a deep pot. Add enough water to just cover birds. Simmer for 45 minutes. Serve hot.

Abalone with Ginseng and Peppercorns

COOKING TIME: 1 HOUR   SERVES 4

This princely concoction will make you weep with pleasure if you do it right, and without the slightest regard for economy. Canned abalone is generally expensive, but even more costly is its dried counterparts, which many Chinese medicinal shops sell. The greatest downside of dried abalone, however, is the lengthy and fiddly processing required before cooking. While the price of ginseng has the sky for its limit, there is always the option of using lower grade ginseng that will not break the bank.

Ingredients

Canned abalone	450 g, drained and thinly sliced
Ginseng	30 g
White peppercorns	1 Tbsp
Water	750 ml
Salt	2 tsp

Method

- Combine all ingredients in a small casserole. Make sure abalone slices are submerged. Cover and simmer for about 1 hour or until abalone is tender.
- If you wish to thicken the gravy a little, add 1 tsp corn flour (cornstarch) dissolved in water at the end of cooking time.

Opposite: Abalone with Ginseng and Peppercorns.

Eucommia Bark with Chicken and Pork

COOKING TIME: 1 HOUR   SERVES 4

Eucommia bark is identifiable by the silvery-white, floss-like shreds that are exposed in the crevices of its dried, cracked surface. Those very shreds are reputed to be good for aiding recovery from back and spinal ailments. It is one of the most popular herbs among herbal chefs.

Ingredients

Chicken	1, about 700 g
Lean pork	300 g, cut into large chunks and excess fat trimmed
Eucommia bark (*du zhong/dou chong*)	20 g
Water	1 litre
Salt	2 tsp

Method

- Clean chicken. Remove all evidence of marrow and blood. Cut into large joints.
- Combine all ingredients in a pot. Simmer for 1 hour. Serve as a savoury soup with a meal.

Chicken and Mushrooms with Chinese Angelica and Astragalus Root in Wine

COOKING TIME: 1 HOUR   SERVES 4

A masterly blend of chicken, herbs, mushrooms and wine, this makes for an extremely 'warming' dish, particularly for new mothers because the Chinese angelica and astragalus root help to replenish the vital essences of the liver and heart. Although there is quite a lot of wine, most of the alcohol evaporates after boiling and can be drunk by even the strictest teetotaler.

Ingredients

Chicken	1, about 900 g
Dried Chinese mushrooms	8
Chinese angelica (*dang gui/dong kwai*)	30 g, rinsed
Astragalus root (*huang qi/puk kei*)	30 g, rinsed
Chinese cooking wine (*hua diao/fa dew*)	500 ml
Water	500 ml
Salt	2 tsp

Method

- Clean chicken thoroughly. Cut into 8 joints. Remove excess fatty skin or skin entirely if you prefer a clear soup.
- Soak mushrooms in hot water until very soft. Trim off hard stalks. Keep whole or slice each into two if very large.
- Place rinsed herbs at the bottom of a pot. Add all other ingredients. Simmer over low heat for 1 hour. Adjust to taste with more salt if needed.

Cooking Know-how

If you souse the chicken in half the amount of wine allowed, the resulting cooked chicken will be much more flavourful.

Opposite: Chicken and Mushrooms with Chinese Angelica and Astragalus Root in Wine.

Dried Cuttlefish and Pork Ribs with Lotus Root Soup

COOKING TIME: 1 HOUR   SERVES 4

Stewed long and lovingly, this soup has a near-perfect combination of flavours. Do not be put off by the coating of mud you see on lotus roots sold at wet markets. This actually means that they are fresh as can be, and they only need to be washed and scraped of the brown skin before cooking.

Ingredients

Cleaned lotus root	400 g, diagonally cut into 1-cm thick slices and soaked in cold water
Dried cuttlefish	150 g, washed
Pork ribs	400 g, washed and excess fat trimmed
Water	1.5 litres
Salt	1 tsp
Light soy sauce	1 Tbsp

Method

- Use kitchen scissors to cut cuttlefish into 1-cm wide pieces. Remove each hard bit that connects the tentacles and body. Snip tentacles into similarly sized pieces.
- Combine all ingredients in a pot. Simmer for 1 hour. Adjust to taste with seasoning. Serve hot.

Cooking Know-how

If you are using dried lotus root slices, soak them for at least several hours or overnight before cooking.

Pig's Tripe with Peppercorns

COOKING TIME: 3–4 HOURS   SERVES 4

Served on the premise of restoring post-natal weakness, this rich stew has been coaxed down the throats of many new mothers. The infusion of lots of peppercorns helps to restore the body's 'heat' and Qi believed to be lost in the process of child-bearing.

Ingredients

Precooked pig's tripe	300 g
White peppercorns	250 g, washed
Water	2 litres
Salt	2 tsp

Method

- Place peppercorns in stomach cavity. Sew up with thread to secure.
- Combine all ingredients in a pot. Stew over low heat for 3–4 hours.

Cooking Know-how

If precooked tripe is unavailable, buy 1 set of pig's tripe from the butcher and clean it yourself at home. Wash pieces inside and out with plenty of salt until they are no longer slimy to the touch. Drain. Heat a dry wok until smoking, then singe tripe pieces thoroughly. An optional step, add 1 tsp bicarbonate of soda to lightly bleach pieces. When done, with pieces partially cooked, remove from wok, wash again and drain.

This recipe can also be double-boiled, which takes about 3 hours, or pressure cooked, which takes about 1 hour 30 minutes. Halve the specified amount of water to 1 litre for either method.

Opposite: Dried Cuttlefish and Pork Ribs with Lotus Root Soup.

Duck and Dried Oysters with Chinese Wolfberries and Lotus Seeds

COOKING TIME: 2 HOURS 30 MINUTES   SERVES 4

This is a magnificent dish for the flavours it encapsulates. Be warned, however, that you will end up with at least 300 ml of duck fat, although it can be skimmed off easily, especially if you refrigerate to allow coagulation. The dish, in fact, tastes better the next day, after it has been clarified.

Ingredients

Duck	1 whole, about 2 kg
Dark soy sauce	2 Tbsp
Cooking oil	3 Tbsp
Dried oysters	15, soaked in hot water and drained
Precooked lotus seeds	30
Chinese wolfberries (*gou qi zi/gei chi*)	2 Tbsp
Chinese cooking wine (*hua diao/fa diew*) (optional)	2 Tbsp
Oyster sauce	2 Tbsp
Sugar	1 tsp
Salt	2 tsp
Water	2 litres

Method

- Clean duck thoroughly. Pat dry with kitchen paper. Remove only webbed feet. If you are confident of the task — believe me, it requires the utmost skill to do it — debone the whole duck so it resembles a deflated balloon. Rub all over with dark soy sauce. Allow to dry.
- Heat half the oil in a non-stick wok. Singe duck all over until skin is brown and taut. Set aside. This step is not compulsory, but it does make the dish look more appetising by leading to a rich brown colour; it is otherwise pale beige.
- Heat remaining oil. Add dried oysters, lotus seeds and wolfberries. Fry for 1–2 minutes. Add wine, oyster sauce, sugar, salt, and just enough water to bind the mixture to a suitable thickness for stuffing.
- Allow mixture to cool slightly, then stuff into duck. Sew up with thread to seal cavity. Place in a deep casserole. Spread excess stuffing around duck. Add water. If liquid seems a bit pale, add 1 Tbsp dark soy sauce mixed with 1 Tbsp oyster sauce. Cover and simmer for 2 hours. Check occasionally. Add more water if needed.

Cooking Know-how

The reason for even suggesting deboning duck is that you can then tuck the whole fowl into a pressure cooker. With bones intact, a duck is generally too long to fit into a standard pressure cooker.

Bean Curd Sticks and Gingko Nuts with Eggs

COOKING TIME: 2 HOURS   SERVES 4

Ingredients

Bean curd sticks (*fu zhu/fu chok*)	150 g, soaked until soft
Precooked gingko nuts	40
Rock sugar	150 g
Water	1 litre
Eggs	2

Method

- Cut soft bean curd sticks into 5-cm pieces. Wash and drain.
- If precooked gingko nuts are unavailable, soak dried ones in water until soft. Remove skins and bitter cores if necessary.
- Except eggs, combine all other ingredients in a pot. Simmer for 2 hours. Just before serving, crack eggs into a bowl and swirl into soup. Stir gently to break yolks. Serve hot or cold.

Opposite: Bean Curd Sticks and Gingko Nuts with Eggs.

Mutton Soup with Barley, Chinese Angelica and Wolfberries

COOKING TIME: 1–2 HOURS   SERVES 4

Combining mutton and Chinese angelica promises to give much nourishment and 'warmth'. The hearty flavours here are tempered by the addition of barley and Chinese wolfberries, both of which are very subtle-tasting. Barley is, in fact, quite bland but acts as a foil for rich gravies, absorbing the incorporated flavours.

Ingredients

Mutton	450 g, cleaned and cut into large chunks
Chinese angelica (*dang gui/dong kwai*)	30 g, thinly sliced
Chinese wolfberries (*gou qi zi/gei chi*)	2 Tbsp
Barley	100 g, washed and drained
Water	1 litre
Salt	2 tsp
Ground black pepper	1/2 tsp

Method

- Combine all ingredients in a deep pot. Cover and simmer for 1–2 hours.
- Add more liquid if necessary. Adjust to taste with seasoning. Serve piping hot for the smell of mutton is stronger when cold.

Euryale Seeds and Longan

COOKING TIME: 1 HOUR 30 MINUTES; SERVES 4

The euryale seed looks like a small corn kernel but performs a strange feat when cooked. Each seed opens up into a little flower of sorts and has a texture and taste not unlike barley. This recipe makes a sweet soup that can be drunk at any time but is reputed to be good for ailments of the spleen and even gonnorhoea. It is also a variation of the longan tea so loved by the Straits Chinese, or Peranakan, community as a pre-meal drink. Served chilled, it is a light dessert with the euryale seeds providing lots of crunch.

Method

- Combine all ingredients in a pot. Simmer over low heat for 1 hour 30 minutes.

Cooking Know-how

This recipe also can be prepared by pressure cooking for 45 minutes with 1 litre water. The amount of water added really depends on how light or rich you want the drink to be.

Ingredients

Euryale seeds (*qian shi/see sat*)	100 g, washed
Dried longan flesh	200 g, washed and thoroughly cleaned
Screwpine (*pandan*) leaves	2, washed and tied into a knot
Rock sugar	150 g
Water	1.5 litres

Opposite: Euryale Seeds and Longan.

Oxtail with Carrots and Eucommia Bark

COOKING TIME: 2 HOURS   SERVES 4

Eucommia bark is reputedly good for the kidneys, liver and ligaments. An unusual-looking ingredient, it gives a real boost to a dish already rich from the oxtail. The carrots and red dates add subtle sweetness.

Ingredients

Oxtail	700 g, cut into large chunks and excess fat and gristle trimmed
Large carrot	1, cut into chunks
Dried red dates (*hong zao/hung cho*)	10, pitted
Eucommia bark (*du zhong/dou chong*)	15 g
Salt	2 tsp
Water	2 litres

Method

- Combine all ingredients in a pot. Cover and simmer over low heat for about 2 hours or until flesh falls off the bone.

Double-cooked Pork with Apricot Kernels and Lotus Seeds

COOKING TIME: 1 HOUR   SERVES 4

Double-cooking pork is a favourite method of the northern Chinese. To first deep-fry the pork and then braise it achieves near-perfect texture and flavour. Deep frying the pork acts to seal in flavour and also renders the pork skin a nice crunchy brown. The subsequent braising tenderises the meat fibres, and the cooked pork breaks apart into tasty shreds. This recipe uses both sweet and bitter apricot kernels, as well as lotus seeds for bulk. It is delicious with plain boiled or steamed rice.

Ingredients

Belly pork	1 piece, about 900 g
Dark soy sauce	2 Tbsp
Salt	2 tsp
Sweet apricot kernels (*nan xing/nam hung*)	10, washed and drained
Bitter apricot kernels (*bei xing/puk hung*)	10, washed and drained
Precooked lotus seeds	40, washed and drained
Water	1.5 litres
Cooking oil for deep-frying	

Method

- Wash and dry belly pork. Make deep scores on the skin about 2 cm apart. Rub all over with soy sauce and salt. Set aside for 1 hour.
- Heat oil for deep-frying. Fry pork for 2 minutes. Drain off as much oil as possible on kitchen paper.
- Combine all ingredients in a deep casserole. Braise for about 1 hour. If the apricot kernels prove too bitter, adjust to taste with 1 tsp sugar. Serve with rice.

Opposite: Oxtail with Carrots and Eucommia Bark.

Chicken with Mushrooms and Chinese Wolfberries

COOKING TIME: 1 HOUR   SERVES 4

A light and delicious soup that has a subtle sweetness from the Chinese wolfberries. Use trimmed and skinned chicken for optimum results.

Ingredients

Chicken	1, about 900 g
Dried Chinese mushrooms	8, soaked until soft and stalks discarded
Chinese wolfberries (gou qi zi/gei chi)	2 Tbsp
Water	1 litre
Salt	2 tsp
Ground black pepper	$^1/_2$ tsp
Fresh coriander (cilantro) leaves	

Method

- Clean chicken thoroughly. Remove head, neck and feet. Do not use gizzard for this soup.
- Except pepper and coriander, combine all other ingredients in a pot. Simmer for 1 hour. Serve with pepper and coriander.

Braised Belly Pork with Chestnuts and Chinese Wolfberries

COOKING TIME: 1 HOUR 30 MINUTES   SERVES 4

The flavours of this dish make it rather similar to those of duck braised in soy sauce. Pork, however, is far less distinctive in taste than duck and also takes less time to cook. This dish is delicious when served with Chinese steamed buns (man tou/man tau) or plain steamed rice. Chinese wolfberries are famous for maintaining good eyesight.

Ingredients

Belly pork with skin on	900 g
Ground white pepper	1 tsp
Salt	2 tsp
Dark soy sauce	2 Tbsp
Cooking oil	3 Tbsp
Dried chestnuts	30, boiled and skins rubbed off
Chinese wolfberries (gou qi zi/gei chi)	2 Tbsp
Cinnamon stick	1, about 8-cm long
Star anise	2
Water	1.5 litres

Method

- Clean pork. Use a sharp knife to score the side of lean meat lengthways (lengthwise); score only as far as the lean meat extends. Pork piece should be divided into 2–3 strips, where each strip is about 3-cm wide. This facilitates slicing after cooking.
- Rub prepared pork with pepper, salt and soy sauce. Let stand for 30 minutes.
- Heat oil. Fry pork over high heat to singe and shrink. Remove and set aside. In remaining oil, fry prepared chestnuts, Chinese wolfberries, cinnamon stick and star anise for 2 minutes. Add water and pork. Cover and simmer for about 1 hour.

Cooking Know-how

This recipe can also be simmered in a pressure cooker. Reduce water to 750 ml and cook for 8–10 minutes at the pressure setting for meats. Do not overcook or chestnuts will disintegrate.

Opposite: Braised Belly Pork with Chestnuts and Chinese Wolfberries.

Dried Scallops, Brown Marrow and Pork Ribs

COOKING TIME: 1 HOUR   SERVES 4

Although dried scallops are not quite in the category of herbal ingredients, they are nevertheless sold by medicinal shops and top quality ones can sometimes be worth their weight in gold. Brown pieces the size of marshmallows, dried scallops impart a beautiful flavour to whatever soup or stew you add them to.

Ingredients

Dried scallops (*gan bei/kong yu chi*)	6, boiled until broken into shreds then drained
Large brown marrow	1, peeled, seeded and cut into 3-cm thick rings
Pork ribs	300 g, washed
Water	1.5 litres
Salt	2 tsp
Ground black pepper	$1/2$ tsp

Method

- Except pepper, combine all other ingredients in a pot. Simmer for about 1 hour. Serve hot with pepper.

Chicken Stuffed with Codonopsis Root

COOKING TIME: 2 HOURS   SERVES 4

White in colour, this stew is eaten for its reputed efficacy gained from the codonopsis root. Slightly different from the standard double-boiled chicken dish, of which diners usually only drink the broth and toy with the chicken, this recipe utilises the slow-braising process that renders the chicken tender without robbing it of its flavour, and also produces a broth that is undeniably rich.

Ingredients

Chicken	1, about 900 g
Salt	2 tsp
Codonopsis root (*dang shen/dong sam*)	100 g
Water	1.5 litres

Method

- Clean chicken thoroughly, inside and out. Pat dry with kitchen paper. Rub with salt. Stuff cavity with codonopsis root. Place in a deep casserole. Add water.
- Cover and braise over low heat for 2 hours. Check liquid level every 30 minutes or so. Add boiling water if necessary.

Cooking Know-how

This recipe can also be pressure cooked. In so doing, halve the amount of liquid used to 750 ml and also cooking time.

Dried Scallops and Pig's Tripe with Chinese Wolfberries

COOKING TIME: 2 HOURS   SERVES 4

Most supermarkets sell precooked tripe that saves you bags of time. The recipe is for a very rich soup that, despite the inexpensive tripe, brooks no stinging on good ingredients like dried scallops. The soup is believed to restore Qi and also counter general malaise after childbirth.

Ingredients

Dried scallops (*gan bei/kong yu chi*)	4, boiled until broken into shreds and drained
Precooked pig's tripe	450 g, washed and cut into bite-sized pieces
Chinese wolfberries (*gou qi zi/gei chi*)	2 Tbsp
Ground white pepper	2 tsp
Salt	2 tsp
Water	1 litre

Method

- Combine all ingredients in a pot. Simmer for 2 hours. Add liquid if necessary.

Cooking Know-how

Aside from stove-top simmering, this recipe can also be double-boiled or pressure cooked. Double-boiling will take about 3 hours, while pressure cooking shortens cooking time to 1 hour. Also, halve the specified amount of water to 500 ml if pressure cooking.

Duck with Chinese Honeyed Dates and Tangerine Peel

COOKING TIME: 2 HOURS   SERVES 4

Not frequently used in savoury cooking, Chinese honeyed dates are, as the name implies, dates preserved in honey. With poultry like duck, however, a touch of sweetness from the dates and the zest of tangerine peel works to temper the bird's rich oiliness, much like how orange does in the classic French duck l'orange. Here, the different flavours blend beautifully after prolonged slow cooking.

Ingredients

Duck	1, about 1.5 kg
Chinese honeyed dates (*mi zao/mutt cho*)	4
Dried tangerine peel	3 pieces
Salt	2 tsp
Water	2 litres

Method

- Clean duck thoroughly. Cut into large joints. Remove every bit of skin and fat from the regions of the neck and breast. Remove parson's nose, especially the glands on either side.
- Combine all ingredients in a pot. Simmer for about 2 hours. At the end of cooking time, liquid in the pot should have halved.

Cooking Know-how

This recipe can be pressure cooked, which means that the amount of water can be reduced by as much as half, as long as all of the duck joints are covered by liquid.

Opposite: Duck with Chinese Honeyed Dates and Tangerine Peel.

Mushrooms with Chestnuts and Lily Bulb Petals

COOKING TIME: 1 HOUR   SERVES 4

A richer and more nourishing version of the classic Cantonese braised mushrooms, this dish is much more substantial with the addition of chestnuts. Imparting fragrance and lightness to the dish, lily bulb petals balance the richness of the mushrooms and chestnuts. Sometimes, lettuce is used in place of chestnuts.

Ingredients

Dried Chinese mushrooms	20, soaked until soft and with stalks discarded
Dried chestnuts	20, boiled for 10 minutes, with skins rubbed off when cooled, then washed and drained
Dried lily bulb petals (*bai he/bak hup*)	15 g
Belly pork	1 piece, about 100 g
Oyster sauce	2 Tbsp
Water	750 ml
Sugar	1 tsp
Salt	1 tsp

Method

- Combine all ingredients in a non-stick pot or casserole. Add enough water to completely cover ingredients. Simmer for 1 hour. Add water if necessary.

Cooking Know-how

If you dislike the fatty taste of belly pork, substitute with a tablespoon of corn or peanut oil.

Duck with Chinese Angelica and Wine

COOKING TIME: 2–3 HOURS   SERVES 4

Some believe that the richness of duck should be tempered with a stuffing of some kind, but in this case, the Chinese angelica and rose wine form a formidable combination in counteracting the flavourful effects of the duck. When buying duck, choose one that has the least fat around the nose area and remember to remove this extremity.

Ingredients

Duck	1, about 2 kg
Dark soy sauce	3 Tbsp
Salt	2 tsp
Chinese angelica (*dang gui/dong kwai*)	60 g
Chinese rose wine (*mei gui lu/mui gwai lo*)	2 Tbsp
Ground white pepper	1 tsp
Sugar	2 tsp
Water	1.5 litres

Method

- Clean duck thoroughly. Pat dry with kitchen paper. Rub all over with dark soy sauce and salt.
- Heat a dry non-stick wok. Singe duck all over until skin is brown and taut. Transfer to a deep pot.
- Add all remaining ingredients. Bring to the boil. Cover and simmer for 2–3 hours.
- Before serving, skim off as much fat as you can from the surface.

Cooking Know-how

Chinese rose wine is, as the name suggests, a wine infused with rose essence or extract and is absolutely delicious when used in conjunction with meat or poultry.

Opposite: Mushrooms with Chestnuts and Lily Bulb Petals.

Steamed Winter Melon with Crabmeat, Chestnuts, Lotus Seeds and Barley

COOKING TIME: 2 HOURS   SERVES 4

Here is a rich change from the simple winter melon soup commonly served at the end of a Chinese banquet. Dried scallops were included in this recipe purely for added flavour, while crab in the recipe can be replaced with other shellfish if desired. Regard winter melon as a blank canvas and create your own masterpiece.

Ingredients

Winter melon	1 whole, about 1.5 kg
Dried scallops (*gan bei/kong yu chi*)	3
Fresh crabmeat	200 g
Dried lotus seeds	20, boiled, cored and with skins rubbed off
Dried chestnuts	20, boiled, cored and with skins rubbed off
Barley	4 Tbsp
Salt	2 tsp
Ground white pepper	1 tsp

Method

- Peel winter melon. Slice off about three-eighths from one end. At the other end, slice off just enough so melon can sit on a plate without wobbling. Remove melon seeds. Scoop out enough melon flesh to leave about 2-cm thickness throughout. Be careful not to make a hole.
- Boil dried scallops in 200 ml water for 15 minutes. Drain scallop pieces. Reserve stock.
- Combine all ingredients in a container. Add enough scallop stock to thoroughly moisten all ingredients.
- Tightly pack combined ingredients into melon bowl. With open end facing up, place melon bowl on a plate. Steam for 2 hours.
- When done, place a serving plate over melon. Very carefully turn over. What you have will be a pale winter melon sphere cupped over its stuffing.
- To serve, bring melon sphere to the table. Cut down along its side to reveal the gems of your creation. You will be admired for your culinary skills.

Chicken with Ginseng and Lotus Root Soup

COOKING TIME: 1 HOUR   SERVES 4

This parent stem of the famous lotus seeds has a peculiar and unique texture and taste. Cantonese cooks treat lotus root in many ways, one of which is to deep-fry slices of the root and then fill the holes with glutinous rice.

Ingredients

Chicken	1, about 700 g
Ginseng	20 g
Lotus root	300 g, thoroughly cleaned and diagonally cut into 1-cm thick slices
Water	1 litre
Salt	2 tsp
Ground white pepper	1 tsp

Method

- Combine all ingredients in a pot. Simmer for 1 hour.

Cooking Know-how

If you have a slight distaste for lotus root, then it is most likely caused by the minute amount of sap that clings to the root. The effect of the sap, however, vanishes if slices of the root are thoroughly cooked through. Another way to ensure the sap's removal is to blanch slices of the root in plenty of boiling water for several minutes prior to cooking and then drain.

Opposite: Chicken with Ginseng and Lotus Root Soup.

Chicken Broth with Barley, Euryale and Lotus Seeds

COOKING TIME: 1 HOUR   SERVES 4

Ingredients

Chicken	1, about 900 g
Barley	3 Tbsp, washed
Euryale seeds	
(*qian shi/see sat*)	15 g, washed
Precooked lotus seeds	40, washed
Water	1 litre
Salt	2 tsp
Ground white pepper	$^1/_2$ tsp

Method

- Clean chicken thoroughly. Remove head and feet. Leave whole.
- Combine all ingredients in a pot. Simmer for 1 hour or until chicken is fork-tender.

Chicken with Gingko Nuts, Lotus Seeds and Chinese Wolfberries

COOKING TIME: 1 HOUR 30 MINUTES   SERVES 4

I have experimented with duck, pork and chicken for this recipe and recommend the lattermost as the perfect foil for the rich compote of ingredients and redolent gravy. The work of Chinese wine and wolfberries give this dish its wonderful flavour.

Ingredients

Chicken	1, about 900 g
Dark soy sauce	2 Tbsp
Salt	1 tsp
Cooking oil	2 Tbsp
Chinese wolfberries	
(*gou qi zi/gei chi*)	2 Tbsp
Chinese cooking wine	
(*hua diao/fa diew*)	2 Tbsp
Oyster sauce	2 Tbsp
Ground white pepper	1 tsp
Salt	1 tsp
Water	1 litre
Precooked gingko nuts	40
Precooked lotus seeds	40

Method

- Clean chicken thoroughly. Rub all over with dark soy sauce and salt. Let stand for 30 minutes.
- Heat oil. Fry chicken over high heat until skin is brown. Remove and drain.
- Transfer remaining oil to a large, glazed clay pot with a snug-fitting lid. Fry wolfberries for 1–2 minutes. Add all seasonings and water. Bring to the boil. Add fried chicken. Simmer over low heat for 40 minutes. Turn once or twice so the chicken's thick parts cook through.
- Add gingko nuts and lotus seeds. Simmer for 15 minutes more. If gravy seems pale, add 1 Tbsp dark soy sauce. Adjust to taste with a dash of oyster sauce or more salt if desired.

Opposite: Chicken with Gingko Nuts, Lotus Seeds and Chinese Wolfberries.

Mixed Meat Hotpot with Lotus Seeds and Chrysanthemum

COOKING TIME: 1 HOUR   SERVES 4

This is a lovely variation of the standard steamboat, with beef, mutton and chicken slices perfumed by chrysanthemum petals. It can also be served steamboat style with all the ingredients assembled for guests to individually select and, in the process, create their own flavours. Lotus seeds and chrysanthemum combine to make a very potent 'cooling' agent.

Ingredients

Beef fillet	200 g, thinly sliced
Lean mutton	200 g, thinly sliced
Skinned chicken breasts	2, thinly sliced
Precooked lotus seeds	30
Water or stock	2 litres
Dried chrysanthemum petals	30 g
Salt	2 tsp or more to taste
Ground white pepper	to taste

Method

- Arrange beef, mutton and chicken slices on separate plates. Then, arrange plates around steamboat or fondue pot at table's centre. Divide lotus seeds into several bowls to be placed around the table.
- Bring water or stock to the boil. Steep dried chrysanthemum for 15 minutes, then strain and discard. Add salt.
- Guests may now do their own cooking and seasoning at the table. The soup at the end of the meal will be very rich, and you can temper it by tossing in vegetables like thinly sliced Chinese cabbage.

Beef and Yam with Ginseng, Chinese Yam and Wolfberries

COOKING TIME: 1 HOUR 30 MINUTES   SERVES 4

This dish will stoke the fires of a flagging system. A 'warming' and substantial dish, it helps to restore the body's 'heat'. Add a handful of Chinese mushrooms for a smoky flavour.

Ingredients

Sirloin steak	700 g, cut into large chunks
Chinese yam (*shan yao/wai san*)	15 g, rinsed and drained
Chinese wolfberries (*gou qi zi/gei chi*)	1 Tbsp, rinsed and drained
Water	1.5 litres
Salt	2 tsp
Yam	200 g, peeled and cut into large chunks

Method

- Except yam, combine all other ingredients in a pot. Bring to the boil. Lower heat. Simmer for 1 hour.
- Add yam. Simmer for 30 minutes more. The yam pieces will render the gravy quite thick.

Opposite: Beef and Yam with Ginseng, Chinese Yam and Wolfberries.

Fish with Cordyceps and Chinese Wolfberries

COOKING TIME: 1 HOUR   SERVES 4

Fish is one ingredient that does not feature frequently in Chinese herbal cooking but is, nevertheless, touted as being beneficial to liver and kidney functions when combined with cordyceps. Chinese wolfberries are known for their efficacy in improving eyesight. The best kinds of fish to use are those species that have firm, relatively boneless meat. Garoupa and threadfin are recommended for this hearty soup.

Ingredients

Garoupa or threadfin	450 g
Cordyceps (*dong chong xia cao/dong chong cho*)	15 g, rinsed
Chinese wolfberries (*gou qi zi/gei chi*)	1 Tbsp, rinsed
Water	800 ml
Chinese cooking wine (*hua diao/fa dew*)	3 Tbsp
Salt	2 tsp

Method

- Cut off fish head. Make several deep cuts along the body, almost to the bone. Leave large, central bone intact but remove as many small bones as possible. Wash and drain thoroughly.
- Combine rinsed ingredients and water in a pot. Cover and simmer for 40 minutes. When done, volume should be reduced to about three quarters. Remove from heat.
- Add fish, wine and salt. Jiggle pot a little to incorporate. Cover and simmer for 15 minutes more.

Abalone and Chicken with Chinese Yam

COOKING TIME: 1 HOUR   SERVES 4

This is a dish fit for emperors, and it pays to use the best abalone you can afford. The chicken, even when skinned, provides enough fat to give the dish a 'smoothness' the Cantonese appreciate, as reflected in their term for it — wat. Chinese yam is a tonic for kidneys and lungs and, at the same time, aids urinary functions. Canned abalone is perfectly acceptable as dried ones take forever to process.

Ingredients

Precooked abalone	300 g, thinly sliced
Skinned chicken	1, about 900 g
Chinese yam (*shan yao/wai san*)	10 slivers
Water	1 litre
Salt	2 tsp
Ground black pepper	1 tsp

Method

- Lightly tenderise abalone slices with blunt edge of a cleaver. Wash and drain slices.
- Clean chicken. Leave whole or cut into 4 large joints.
- Place Chinese yam in a pot. Add all other ingredients over the top. Cover and simmer over low–medium heat for 1 hour. Check occasionally to see if more liquid needs to be added.
- When done, the chicken should fall off the bone, and abalone just tender enough.

Opposite: Fish with Cordyceps and Chinese Wolfberries.

Buddha's Feast

COOKING TIME: 1 HOUR   SERVES 8

Better known to the Chinese as luo han zai *in Mandarin or* lor hawn chai *in Cantonese, this is a favourite festive dish. The recipe requires a lot of pre-cooking preparation, but the flavours that blend so beautifully and emerge the day after it is cooked, which is incidentally the best time to serve it, makes it all worthwhile. If you cannot get all the ingredients listed here, modify as you please without cutting down too much on the number of ingredients. Traditionally, it should contain 18 different ingredients, each symbolic of the 18* luo han *or disciples of Buddha.*

Do not confuse sweetened bean curd wafers, also known as teem chok *in Cantonese, with bean curd sticks, or* fu chok. *The former are perfectly rectangular, wafer-sized, coffee-coloured pieces, while the latter are irregularly shaped, pale-yellow sticks.*

Ingredients

Precooked gingko nuts	40, washed and thoroughly drained, as well as cored if necessary
Precooked lotus seeds	40, washed and thoroughly drained, as well as cored if necessary
Dried Chinese mushrooms	12, soaked until soft and stalks discarded
Chinese cabbage	300 g, cut into 5-cm long pieces, washed and drained
Sweetened bean curd wafers (*tian zhu/ teem chok*)	4, cut into 5-cm long pieces, soaked until soft and drained
Dried lily buds (golden needles)	100 g, soaked until soft, each tied into a firm knot and with hard tips cut off
Dried red dates (*hong zao/hung cho*)	20, pitted and washed
Cloud ear fungus (*yun er/wun yi*)	3 Tbsp, soaked until soft, washed and drained
Canned button mushrooms	200 g, drained
Canned straw mushrooms	200 g, drained
Transparent vermicelli (*fen si/fun see*)	60 g, soaked until soft
Black hair moss (*fa cai/fat choy*)	15 g, soaked, thoroughly cleaned and drained
Ginger	1 large knob, about 60 g
Preserved red bean curd (*nan ru/nam yu*)	4–6 pieces
Hoisin sauce	3 Tbsp
Oyster sauce	3 Tbsp
Sugar	1 Tbsp
Water	2 litres
Cooking oil for deep-frying	

Method

- The traditional way of preparing this dish involved separately deep-frying all the ingredients, except the mushrooms, vermicelli, black hair moss and seasonings, in a wok of hot oil. This step, however, can be eliminated if you do not like the dish oily.
- If you chose to deep-fry, remove bulk of oil until 3 Tbsp remain. Bruise ginger with skin on. Add to wok. Fry ginger until fragrant, then push aside. Add preserved red bean curd. Mash with spatula and sauté quickly.
- Except sugar and water, add all other ingredients. Toss thoroughly. When well mixed, add sugar and water. Cover and simmer for about 1 hour.
- Adjust to taste by adding more preserved bean curd (for saltiness), hoisin sauce (for flavour) and/or oyster sauce (for richness). Do not add any salt. Add water if necessary. Consistency should be that of a thick stew.

Cooking Know-how

To deep-fry successfully, the oil has to be smoking hot and the ingredients to be fried have to be completely dry. Place only one ingredient on a wire ladle before lowering into hot oil. When done, drain.

Chicken with Chestnuts and Chinese Wolfberries

COOKING TIME: 1 HOUR   SERVES 4

For this dish, use a larger than normal chicken as anything less is likely to break up after long stewing or braising.

Ingredients

Chicken	1, about 1.5 kg
Dark soy sauce	2 Tbsp
Salt	3 tsp
Cooking oil	4 Tbsp
Dried chestnuts	30, boiled for 15 minutes, with skins rubbed off when cooled, then washed and drained
Chinese wolfberries (*gou qi zi/gei chi*)	1 Tbsp
Oyster sauce	3 Tbsp
Ground white pepper	1 tsp
Water	1.5 litres
Iceberg lettuce	1 head

Method

- Clean chicken thoroughly. Leave head and neck intact. Drain. Rub all over with dark soy sauce and 1 tsp salt. Let stand for 15 minutes.
- Heat oil. Fry chicken over high heat. Remove when well browned all over. Leave to cool.
- In remaining oil, fry chestnuts for 3 minutes. Add remaining salt, wolfberries, oyster sauce, pepper, and a few Tbsp water. When mixture is almost dry, remove and stuff into chicken. Sew up with thread to seal cavity. Place in a deep casserole. Arrange excess stuffing around the chicken to be cooked together.
- Pour remaining water over chicken. Cover and simmer for about 1 hour. Add water if necessary. Adjust to taste with 1–2 Tbsp oyster sauce. Be mindful that flavour from the stuffing will eventually seep out and blend with braising liquid.
- If chicken seems underdone, simmer for 30 minutes more. Serve on a bed of lettuce. Leave extra liquid on the side for anyone who likes to mix it with rice.

Dried Scallops, Lotus Seeds and Chinese Angelica in Winter Melon

COOKING TIME: 2 HOURS   SERVES 4

There is simply a variation of the previous recipe with Chinese angelica as the backbone of nourishment. A soupy dish, the winter melon here becomes more like a receptacle. The melon and its contents are steamed in a large steamer with a high, dome-shaped lid. The result is regarded as an extremely nourishing soup, especially for invalids and new mothers.

Ingredients

Dried scallops (*gan bei/kong yu chi*)	4–5
Winter melon	1 whole, about 1.5 kg
Precooked lotus seeds	20
Chinese angelica (*dang gui/dong kwai*)	20 g
Water	600 ml
Salt	2 tsp

Method

- Boil scallops in some water. Drain scallop pieces. Shred if necessary. Reserve stock.
- Cut off top of winter melon. Remove seeds. Scoop out excess flesh until a pot-shaped receptacle remains.
- Fill melon bowl with all ingredients. Add scallop stock and as much water as the melon can hold. Place melon on a deep plate. Steam for 2 hours.

Opposite: Dried Scallops, Lotus Seeds and Chinese Angelica in Winter Melon.

weights and measures

LIQUID AND VOLUME MEASURES

Metric	Imperial	American
5 ml	$1/6$ fl oz	1 teaspoon
10 ml	$1/3$ fl oz	1 dessertspoon
15 ml	$1/2$ fl oz	1 tablespoon
60 ml	2 fl oz	$1/4$ cup (4 tablespoons)
85 ml	$2^1/2$ fl oz	$1/3$ cup
90 ml	3 fl oz	$3/8$ cup (6 tablespoons)
125 ml	4 fl oz	$1/2$ cup
180 ml	6 fl oz	$3/4$ cup
250 ml	8 fl oz	1 cup
300 ml	10 fl oz ($1/2$ pint)	$1^1/4$ cups
375 ml	12 fl oz	$1^1/2$ cups
435 ml	14 fl oz	$1^3/4$ cups
500 ml	16 fl oz	2 cups
625 ml	20 fl oz (1 pint)	$2^1/2$ cups
750 ml	24 fl oz ($1^1/5$ pints)	3 cups
1 litre	32 fl oz ($1^3/5$ pints)	4 cups
1.25 litres	40 fl oz (2 pints)	5 cups
1.5 litres	48 fl oz ($2^2/5$ pints)	6 cups
2.5 litres	80 fl oz (4 pints)	10 cups

LENGTH

Metric	Imperial
0.5 cm	$1/4$ inch
1 cm	$1/2$ inch
1.5 cm	$3/4$ inch
2.5 cm	1 inch

ABBREVIATION

tsp	teaspoon
Tbsp	tablespoon
g	gram
kg	kilogram
ml	millilitre

DRY MEASURES

Metric	Imperial
30 grams	1 ounce
45 grams	$1^1/2$ ounces
55 grams	2 ounces
70 grams	$2^1/2$ ounces
85 grams	3 ounces
100 grams	$3^1/2$ ounces
110 grams	4 ounces
125 grams	$4^1/2$ ounces
140 grams	5 ounces
280 grams	10 ounces
450 grams	16 ounces (1 pound)
500 grams	1 pound, $1^1/2$ ounces
700 grams	$1^1/2$ pounds
800 grams	$1^3/4$ pounds
1 kilogram	2 pounds, 3 ounces
1.5 kilograms	3 pounds, $4^1/2$ ounces
2 kilograms	4 pounds, 6 ounces

OVEN TEMPERATURE

Regulo	°C	°F	Gas
Very slow	120	250	1
Slow	150	300	2
Moderately slow	160	325	3
Moderate	180	350	4
Moderately hot	190/200	370/400	5/6
Hot	210/220	410/440	6/7
Very hot	230	450	8
Super hot	250/290	475/550	9/10